For Lorraine,

Visions from Mary

Love & Blessings!

Michele A. Livington

Visions from Mary

by Michele A. Livingston

Blue Mantle Press

Blue Mantle Press * Virginia Beach * Virginia

Visions from Mary

First printing, April 1999

Book design by The Beigh's Graphic Services
Edited by Kathleen Sparrow
Paintings by Michele A. Livingston

Library of Congress Cataloging-Number 99-60251

ISBN-0-9665485-1-5

In loving memory of my parents
C. Lear Livingston and Dorothy I. Livingston with
respect and gratitude

Acknowledgements

I wish to first thank Mary, the Blessed Mother, for choosing me to be a messenger of Her divine visions and wisdom. I thank Her for Her obedience to be the Mother of Jesus — the Son — and for Her humility, compassion, and undying love for us, Her children.

Next, I acknowledge and thank my wonderful husband and soul partner, Jon Robert Stroh. This book could not have been done without his love, support, and encouragement.

Also to my beautiful mother, Dorothy, now in Heaven, whose presence and love I felt while creating this book. My father, Lear, who I will always remember as a gentle and kind man.

With love and gratitude I wish to thank all those who devoted time and energy to this project: Jane Howard, an "earth angel" who wrote my foreword; Dr. Scott Sparrow who believed in this material and wrote the introduction; his wife Kathleen — my editor — whose enthusiasm, openness, and willingness to accept this work proved to be a great confirmation for me; and to their publishing house Blue Mantle; to Jason and Stephanie Beigh, who spent long hours working on refining the project and preparing it for press; to Jim Rietmulder for his early editing work; to Tonya Geissinger for transcribing; and, for all those who gave me hope over the last five-year period.

Finally, I acknowledge all of the heavenly hosts — archangels Michael, Gabriel, and Raphael who oversee the paintings; Daniel, my angel of inspiration; and all other angels who have come to my aid.

Contents

Foreword

Michele Livingston's exquisite artistic creation — *Visions from Mary* — brought once again to mind St. Gregory Palamas' inspirational words:

"Wishing to create an image of beauty, and to manifest clearly to men and to angels the power of his art, God truly created Mary all-beautiful. He made Her a blending of all perfections — divine, angelic, and human; a sublime beauty adorning two worlds, lifted up from earth to Heaven, and even transcending that."

Michele's transformational art expressed in divinely-inspired paintings and words of grace allows us a heightened perception of the beauty and light of Mary. As you experience *Visions from Mary* you will know that Mary is near, and you will find your heart opening and overflowing with thankfulness for the personal relationship with Mary that is extended to you through Michele's shared visions. I wouldn't be the least bit surprised that, if as you experience this book, the smell of roses fills your room. *Visions from Mary* is a book that awakens the soul's senses!

Michele Livingston is a beautiful woman who has lived and breathed service to Mary since her first vision of Blessed Mother in 1993. Her dedication, commitment, and energy devoted to the Divine Mother is of such purity and goodness that when she shared with me the task Mary had given to her — to write the text and create the paintings for *Visions from Mary* — I thought to myself "Who better?!" Her paintings are visions of divine eloquence spoken through an obedient heart. Her words radiate the light of God.

The book is truly a divinely inspired, healing experience. This book is to be experienced intimately by your soul. It offers images and words to contemplate and meditate upon. It offers an opportunity for "quantum-plation" — contemplating the quantum's of God's love for each of us. It brings an invisible world into visibility.

Visions from Mary is an artistic blessing. Think of how in so many ways we are like lost children. In the midst of confusion, uncertainty, and chaos, we want our simple cry — "I want my Mommy" — to be heard.

It has been through the Divine that Michele Livingston was "commissioned" to bring forth *Visions from Mary* in tangible expression. It is a gift of comfort, peace, hope, and love. Page by page you will feel the Divine Mother draw you closer to Her heart, into Her arms, taking you to Her breast, and whispering to you gently, "I am here. You are not alone. You are loved by God."

Jane M. Howard
Commune with the Angels (A.R.E. Press, 1992)

Michele's Story

I had my first personal vision of the Blessed Mother in September of 1993, shortly after my earthly mother Dorothy had passed away. Dorothy was always drawn to the Blessed Mother, collecting icons and prayer cards of Her. Yet I never had a *personal* attraction to Mother Mary prior to this visitation.

I was in my bedroom and had just finished my prayer and meditation time. I felt a warmth come over me from the crown of my head to the soles of my feet. There was a glow that filled my whole room. Then I saw Her — the Blessed Mother!

She was delicate in appearance with brown hair, parted in the middle, framing a lovely heart-shaped face. She was dressed all in white with blue light emanating from Her.

I could not speak or move. She gently reached out Her hand and said in a soft voice, "Daughter, with you I am well pleased. I have chosen you to paint twelve paintings of my feminine, divine, healing essence. These will be paintings of global interest and healing. I have chosen you, and I am asking that you accept this request."

Assuming Mary was only for Catholics, I asked her, "Why have you come to me? I am not Catholic."

And She said, "I am Mother of you all, and I have aligned with you, my daughter."

Again I questioned Her, "But why have you chosen me?"

Mary smiled and said, "Because of your childlike spirit. Unless we become as children, we cannot enter the Kingdom. You are obedient as a child and you do not question. You have great talent; therefore, the combination of your visionary abilities and creative talent is the combination that will work for this project." Then She left.

I prayed about my experience and waited patiently for Her to return. During that time I reflected upon my life and looked for clues as to why I was chosen. I first reviewed my childhood and the circumstances which gave me life in this world.

It is my belief that life is the gift of love and that all of our lives are miracles. My parents were convinced, though, that I was a *special* miracle! My father — a confirmed bachelor — finally married my mother when he was 50 (she was 44). The third month into their new marriage, she went into the hospital to have a large fibroid tumor removed. That is when they discovered that she was pregnant with me! My mother, a lady of great faith, had prayed for a baby girl for many years. She wasn't about to let anything happen to me. I grew around the tumor and was delivered in 1951, weighing only five pounds, with a curved spine and a clubfoot. The first few years of my life were "touch and go," as I almost died several times.

Yet I was filled with wonder. At age two, the first thing I wanted to do was draw; I also prayed a lot, as my mother recalled. Around age three, I would run through the rooms of our house, fall to my knees, and start to pray! She wasn't sure if I was going to be an artist or a minister!

In elementary school I was often accused of daydreaming. One day in the fourth grade, my teacher was telling the class a story and stopped to ask me what I was staring at. I reported *seeing* the whole scene of the story unfolding around her and described it in great detail. It was then, through the sensitivity of my teacher, that I began to be called *gifted* and was encouraged to use my imagination and see things around people.

Some of those things that I *see* are angels. Throughout my life, I've had many angelic encounters. The first I can vividly remember occurred when I was 14. My father died suddenly from a brain tumor, causing me to become increasingly withdrawn. My mother took part of our savings and sent me to Europe to study art and French, which helped me to heal emotionally. While traveling in Paris one day, Sarah (a classmate) and I became separated from the rest of the group of students, who returned to the university without us. We managed to find the subway, but couldn't remember how to get back. We started to cry and pray!

A mist rolled through the subway, and a tall gentleman, in a white suit with white hair and blue eyes, stepped out of the mist. "Don't cry," he said smiling. He then pointed to his gold badge that said, "International Guide." He said he understood all languages and spoke to us in English. He put us on the right subway car, paid our fare, and rode with us. While we rode along, he seemed to personally know us and told us about our lives. He told Sarah that she was a "perfect student." Then he told me that I needed to study more and to learn patience. We were both astounded!

When we arrived at our destination, the three of us walked out of the subway car. We turned to thank the man in white, only to discover that he simply vanished with the mist. We looked at each other in amazement — *knowing we had witnessed an angel!*

About a year later I had a dream that I was in a large room with many people — all had white hair and white suits. Across the room stood the gentleman who had "saved" us in the subway. He walked over, smiled, and said to me, "Yes, we are all angels here. We are called the *Mercy Band*. We are directed to take human form in times of need. When your prayer was heard, I was sent down!"

As each year passed, I became more sensitive and *aware* of things around myself — and around others. After graduating with a master's degree in art, I taught for ten years in the inner city of Harrisburg, Pennsylvania. It was very challenging. I left that position in 1982 to develop an art business which involved travel throughout the country. This continued for the next ten years. Then in 1991, at the age of 40, a dream became a reality — I opened my own art gallery — "Divine Inspirations"!

At about the same time, I started to become more acutely aware of my spiritual gifts. The Bible lists the gifts of the spirit in at least four places: Romans 12:6-8, I Corinthians 12:7-10, I Corinthians 12:27, 28 and Ephesians 4:11. Spiritual gifts are the natural talents God has given to us. These talents are blessed by His spirit dwelling in our lives. One gift that seemed to develop rapidly at that time for me was the gift of prophecy. Prophecy gives me the opportunity to "uplift, encourage, and ennoble my fellowman" (I Corinthians 14:3). When I pray for people, I experience locutions (hearing words) and see (visions and symbols) in detail around them. This gift is of great help and interest to people. I call this gift "visionary counseling." I am a "spiritual visionary" and feel the *artist in me* greatly enhances my visionary capacities.

Being a student of the Bible, I recognized this as a healing gift. I asked in prayer why some of the gifts of the spirit came to me in later years. The answer I received was, "Everyone to whom much is given, of him will much be required." (Luke 12:48) This means if we are given gifts, we are required to use them wisely. I feel I was not mature or focused enough before age 40 to use the gifts wisely. The gift of discernment came to me later, so that I am protected in the work I do.

I believe that the Creator-God works through me. I also have three angelic helpers I call the "light beings." They tell me three is the number of protection and the Trinity. The light beings always form a triangle around the person or group that I am counseling for protection.

Small children (from approximately ages 1 to 5) "see and hear" the invisible world and tell you all about it. They are in a different energy frequency and can tap into the invisible world. I feel that I return to this frequency when I do my counseling.

I believe that the paintings in this project will heal those who view them and study the lessons and meditations given to me by the Blessed Mother. It is Her healing essence that came through me as I painted, and She directed the creation of each and every one. She even determined the order in which they were painted.

A couple weeks after Her first appearance to me, She visited again and said, "I want 'The Annunciation' painted first." I remembered the event of Gabriel appearing to Mary, announcing that She was to be the Mother of God. (Luke 1:26-28)

Even though Mary might not have needed confirmation — or a divine sign — to answer Her call, I was skeptical at best. But I received the signs that I needed. Throughout the five-year period that the *Visions from Mary* project was conceived and completed, I received many confirmations from our Creator and Mother Mary. They always reminded me that I was "on the right track" and that indeed the project was divinely ordained.

After Mary appeared to give me the title of the upcoming painting, I would receive a confirmation about it. For example the day after She gave me the title "The Annunciation," I received a postcard in the mail from a friend that depicted Gabriel kneeling and handing Mary a white lily with the title "Annunciation" written on the front of the card. Typically, cards of the Annunciation are sent at Christmas and this was in September! My friend said she just liked the image on the postcard and felt inspired to send it.

I received another confirmation about "The Lamb of God." I actually questioned Mary about this one! A week after receiving the title, I was invited to a Catholic mass. Having a Presbyterian background, I didn't know what to expect, but I went anyway. When we entered the pew, I looked down and on the seat was a small golden rose. I picked it up and noticed it was the front of an earring that had been broken off. I clutched it throughout the service, and when we left the cathedral, I was drawn to a beautiful stained glass window. It was a realistic portrayal of Christ holding a lamb. At His feet was a golden primrose bush, with an image identical to the golden rose earring! Written on the bottom border of the window were the words: "Behold the Lamb of God who takes away the sin of the world." I then heard Mary's gentle voice very plainly say, "See my daughter, do not question, I wish 'The Lamb of God' be your next painting!"

A manifestation that cannot be overlooked was my "Madonna of the Towel." Everyday I take time to walk in nature. I then say prayers of thankfulness, prayers for help and guidance, and then spend time listening.

In July of 1996, I was out walking, when I plainly heard Mary say, "You shall now receive the *anointing of healing* in your hands." While I was wondering what She meant, my hands started to grow hotter and hotter. It was not from the hot July weather, but an inner heat that emanated from inside my hands outward. When I returned from my walk that Sunday, I shared the story with my husband while I did laundry. I placed a stack of neatly folded towels in the bathroom, next to the Jacuzzi as I always did. We left shortly after that to get a bite to eat, returning later that evening. When I walked into the bathroom and glanced at the "neatly folded towels," I couldn't believe what I saw! The very top towel had formed into a perfect image of the Madonna holding the baby Jesus! I went over and felt the sculpted towel. It appeared rather hard, as if it were spray starched. It reminded me of the Michelangelo sculpture of the Pieta that I had seen in Rome.

I prayed and asked why the miraculous manifestation occurred. The answer was that the "Madonna of the Towel" was a confirmation for me that indeed I had received the anointing of healing in my hands. I later remembered that Christ took a towel, before He was crucified, and wiped His disciples feet. What a fitting material to use for a miraculous manifestation!

Since then, several miraculous healings have occurred with this gift of healing and the Mary paintings. One was with my cleaning lady, Ruth. After leaving my art gallery in 1997, I hung the Mary paintings in my home office. Ruth was cleaning my office and I heard her gasp. When I came into the room, she started to cry. She told me she had a tumor in her left breast and that she had to have surgery in three days to have it removed. She also said that looking at the paintings made her *feel warm*. I then heard Mother Mary say, "Put your hands on Ruth". When I laid my hands on her the voice said, "The tumor is dissolving." I told Ruth what I was hearing, as healing heat poured out of my hands and into her. About a week later, Ruth called me to say that before she went into surgery, the doctor did a scan for the tumor — and it was gone!

In October of 1997, I was returning from Washington, DC, after giving a lecture. My husband and I stopped at the grotto at Mount St. Mary College in Emmitsburg, Maryland. There were not many people in the grotto as we walked around. It was very peaceful. As we were leaving, I glanced up at the 200-foot high, golden statue of Mary, and above it was the most beautiful *sunbow*. I call it a sunbow because there was no rain in sight. Mary told me that the sunbow is her symbol of hope — not only for me, but for all of humanity. A gentleman next to us took a picture of the statue with the sunbow. I gave him one of my business cards and told him that if he ever had them developed to please send me one.

Several days later Mary announced to me that December was going to be pivotal for moving the project forward. She said,

"December is the twelfth month of the year, and twelve is the number of completion." She also said, "Daughter, watch for a sign from me on December 12 (12/12).

I had totally forgotten about the photographs of the golden statue and the sunbow. But on December 12 I received an envelope from Baltimore, Maryland. Sure enough, the photographs had arrived of the grotto on the very date that Mary told me to watch for a sign! This was the confirmation I needed that this project was on track. (I later found out that this date is the *Feast of Our Lady of Guadalupe*!)

Mary wanted to give humanity a well-rounded concept of Herself and Her Son to ponder through the paintings. Therefore, there are different events portrayed in this series pertaining to the lives of Mary and Jesus. They are the *Annunciation, Nativity, Baptism, Communion, Crucifixion, Resurrection, Descent of the Holy Spirit, Assumption* and *Coronation*. Painting number eight, "The Lamb of God," is a name given to Jesus, and painting number two, "The Mystical Rose," is a title that was given to Mary in the early Christian era. The last of the series, painting number twelve, "The Miraculous Medal," depicts an event that occurred in Paris in 1830. Mary appeared to Catherine Labouré requesting that a medal be struck for protection and healing. It came to be known as the "Miraculous Medal," since many miracles occurred to those who wore it.

Mary did not request a certain medium for the paintings, like watercolor or oil. Therefore, I chose pastel chalk, since it is a flowing medium for me to work in. Before beginning each painting, I would center and pray for guidance. I learned to say the rosary and felt led to say it before starting. Mary did not always appear while I was painting, but I always felt Her presence and heard Her gentle voice through locutions. She instructed me on what colors to use, sometimes saying, "Daughter, pick up blue chalk, now the purple..." and so on. The style of the work was so different from my previous paintings. Each painting took no more than two hours to complete even though they were created on large pastel boards (30 by 40 inches).

It amazed me how fast they were created, for I was only the vehicle to create them. Mary told me many times, "It is not my physical appearance that will be portrayed, but my feminine, divine, healing essence." Therefore, as they progressed I noticed each face, eye color, and profile was unique and different.

Her visitations would occur in different rooms of our home, during my walks in nature, and at night in my dreams. Again, sometimes I didn't see Her, but would feel or hear Her. Occasionally, She even left the scent of roses around me.

The paintings were created over a period of one year — from May 1994 to May of 1995. Then through the end of 1997, I received her messages, lessons, prayers, and meditations for each painting. The Blessed Mother gave these paintings and writings directly to me. I have made every effort to keep them pure and unadulterated.

After the paintings were completed, Mary gave me the order in which She wanted them presented (which was not the same as the order that they were painted). I hung them in this order in my gallery, and did several *Visions from Mary* workshops as the manuscript continued to develop.

In July of 1998, during a meditation, I received the image of archangel Michael. He explained to me that he, along with archangels Gabriel and Raphael, oversee the paintings. Each of them watches over four of the twelve paintings. Michael told me that they would give me an addendum for the book. This information added still another dimension to the project, further enhancing the material already provided by Mary.

The Blessed Mother gave me another message about the project in the beginning of 1998. She simply said, "Daughter, I am very pleased with this project. There will be some controversy about it, but know that I shall stand by you and speak through you, for it is divinely ordained by the Creator, my Son — the Christ, and myself. Blessings and peace be with you."

I feel these transformative and healing paintings will give you the feminine essence of Mary. You can meditate upon the symbols, say the inspiring prayers, and ponder the messages and lessons given by Her, allowing Her to touch your life as She has mine.

She reaches out to all of us with love and hope for global healing. Mary is truly the "Mother of us all."

Michele A. Livingston
December 1998

The Archangels

My communication with the archangels commenced on July 6, 1998. Daniel, the mighty angel of inspiration and creative writing, was assigned to be my liaison with the archangels Michael, Raphael, and Gabriel. Among the many things he conveyed to me was the importance of this project — *Visions from Mary* — for bringing the feminine, divine essence to the world in greater ways. He helped me to adjust to the different energy shifts and patterns that accompanied the presence of the archangels.

Archangel Michael appeared first. Our great room has 18-foot-high ceilings, and archangel Michael looked to be around 12 feet tall, with a very muscular body. He had very rich, deep dark brown hair, that was short and wavy. He had blue eyes, very chiseled features, and high cheekbones. He was stunningly handsome.

The day that Michael appeared to me he wore armor. His V-shaped waist armor pointed toward his thighs, where it met a Roman-looking short skirt, in a beautiful shade of blue. He wore golden sandals, with straps up to his knees. His mighty, white wings stretched almost the width of our great room.

He held in his right hand a gold-hammered shield. He told me:

This is the "shield of protection" for humanity, for I am the archangel of protection.

It was very elaborate, decorated with large sparkling diamonds, beautiful sapphires, rubies, and emeralds. He told me that each gemstone is significant. Diamonds stand for purity of heart, God's creation, and one's spiritual journey. He emphasized that his mission is to help to oversee God's creation and our spiritual journeys, if we let him. The bright blue sapphires on his shield represent the mental processes, our soul-mind communication, and communication with the Creator. He explained that the color royal blue symbolizes speaking one's truth. It also is a color of spiritual calm and peace. Rubies represent the blood that Christ shed for us. They also represent the physical plane of existence. The color red vibrates with the legs and is a grounding color. The legs ground us through gravity to the earth. The emeralds represent our emotions — heart love. They signify emotional cleansing and purification.

In his left hand, Michael carried a mighty golden sword — the *sword of courage*. This is the symbolic sword individuals may visualize in order to move forward in life without fear. Michael uses this sword to symbolically slay those that are not in the light. For he protects the heavenly realms and watches over the souls that are devoted to God.

Michael shared the following message:

I am Michael, the archangel. I was created to oversee the globe — to protect children, to protect animals, to protect the lost, to protect those that need to find their way. I am a mighty archangel. I am at Mary's right arm. The Blessed Mother and I receive souls to the other side when they make transition, for I am also the angel of death. I am prince of light in Heaven.

When one has remained in one's prayer time, and one has a good and pure heart, and one has honored the Blessed Mother, the Christ, and has concerns of the angelic kingdom, then the following occurs:

When they breathe their last breath, the soul leaves through the top of the head, rises above the body and goes through the portal or tunnel into the fourth dimension. The fourth dimension is a higher energy frequency than we are in now. It is very light, it is very airy, and it is very beautiful. As they approach the light, the Christ appears in the center. I am to the right of Christ; Mary is to the left.

When I accompany the Blessed Mother to the earth plane, many times I am at Her right arm. I often announce the coming of our Blessed Mother. I am the one that the children of Medjugorje saw before they saw Mary.

Angels have never been human. They were created to assist mankind on the spiritual journey. They take assignments from the Creator on a daily basis. There are many levels of angels. There are angels of healing, and there are angels of birthing that assist a woman who is about to deliver her child. There are angels of inspiration, like Daniel, who are assigned to various projects. There are also companion or guardian angels that watch over souls. We do what we need to do.

For example, this project — Visions from Mary *— was preordained many, many years ago. We knew that we would be overseeing each of the paintings. I oversee certain ones for specific reasons. This is what Mary, the Queen of the Angels, assigned us to do and also our Heavenly Father, the Creator, assigned us to do.*

Because I am the powerful archangel Michael, I can also split my energy. I can protect those in Bosnia as I communicate with you. I'm able to oversee the mighty archangels as I save a baby from drowning. For an angel is not human; an angel is very condensed energy, with a mind and thought forms that are placed there

by the Creator. Therefore, I go where I am assigned,
and I go where I am needed.

Archangel Michael explained that while I did not paint the paintings in a specific order, it was planned that they be arranged in a specific order. He said that he was to oversee the first part of this book, and to specifically provide information on "The Baptism" (painting number 4), "The Crucifixion" (painting number 6), "The Lamb of God"(painting number 8), and "The Coronation" (painting number 11). He also explained that each of the paintings are dynamic in their own right and each vibrates with a different energy, just as our souls are unique and each soul vibrates with a different energy. The paintings also align with different numbers; therefore, some souls will be affected by some paintings more so than by others. Because of this, numerological information has also been included for each of the paintings.

Archangel Michael also foretold of coming earth changes:

I also oversee earth changes and will be herald-
ing souls into the light that are believers. Those
that are nonbelievers shall not enter the Kingdom,
although they enter the fourth dimension. It is that
simple. I am not here to judge the world, only to
share truth.

The poles will shift. Many glaciers will break off
and move forward. There will be great tidal
waves, and water will cover much of the earth as
you know it. The dry arid lands of the desert will
crack in half, and waters will flow through them.
Many coast lines will be inundated with water to
create new coast lines. Volcanoes will erupt and
lava will flow in magnitude. The sky will darken.

This is what we call the "three days of darkness," for there will be ash and smoke that will rise and block the sun.

Again this is not to put fear in your heart, but to make you aware that everything changes. Everything is constantly moving and evolving. Man has polluted the earth, Mother Earth, our precious land. She now needs cleansing, and this cleansing process must come soon. Many, many souls will be taken to the heavens. It is time now to start thinking about your own immortality.

Many people ask what hell is. Hell is an environment created through one's own fear, anger, greed, and renouncement. It is created by refusing to worship God. For as I stated before, it is quite simple. There are believers, and there are nonbelievers. Believers believe that they were created by a mighty and higher power than themselves which is the godhead. They believe love is the key to win all hearts for the good. Nonbelievers believe only in themselves, or possibly nothing at all. Nonbelievers are again angry, fearful, and live in the shadows, in a form of denial.

Remember, anything that takes you away from your own divinity — your own divine power, the God within you — and anything that distracts or pulls you down from your true empowerment, is not from God.

Nonbelievers cannot enter Heaven because they do not believe there is a Heaven. They do not believe there is a God. They go to a very, very stagnant area where they remain.

Therefore, be wary on your walk through this life-
time that you keep your eye on the mark, that you
keep the goal of Christ and the godhead in front of
you, always striving and reaching farther toward
the ultimate connection. The ultimate connection is
the Source, and the Source is God, and God is love.

My wish for all of you is that you come into the
light now, as soon as possible, and that you will
remain with us in the heavenly realms
forever more.

While archangel Michael's energy was very masculine,
archangel Gabriel appeared very gentle, much softer and more
loving than the other archangels. There was a feminine quality or
essence about Gabriel. He (or she) appeared to me with short
golden waves or locks of hair, pure blue eyes, and very soft delicate
features. He wore a white linen robe. He had bare feet and beautiful,
pure snowy white wings.

Gabriel held a beautiful white lily which he set down as he
spoke to me.

Hello, my blessed daughter Michele. This is Gabriel.
I am here now to talk about the paintings that I oversee,
for they are quite beautiful. I am projecting to you a
more female essence than male. Mary felt more
comfortable with the message of conception and the
birth of Christ coming from a female vibration. So
I was sent to Her for the Annunciation.

When Gabriel finished his introduction, archangel Raphael, the
divine angel of healing, stepped before me. I could feel his very,
gentle energy. He, too, was about twelve feet tall. He wore a
beautiful long, emerald green cape, with a long, white, silky

linen-looking gown underneath, and light brown sandals. His wings were luminescent — absolutely beautiful! They vibrated between pale aqua and chartreuse. His hair was very soft, parted in the middle, and fell to his shoulders. He had hazel green eyes, and a beautiful golden light above his head.

He held a golden staff, and on the top of it was a six-pointed star. He stepped closer and introduced himself:

I am the archangel of divine healing. I heal and soothe the wounds of men. I am charged to heal the earth. I am the mighty angel of prayer, of love, joy, and light. I am the angel of science and knowledge, and of all virtues.

The archangels were charged with protecting and guiding the process of each painting. They went into great detail with the descriptions and the reasons why certain symbols were placed within each painting. As you read *Visions from Mary*, you are promised to receive divine blessings and healing.

Introduction

In the rich tradition of Christian mysticism, Mary, the Mother of Jesus, exemplifies the kind of relationship that all of us can enjoy with the Divine. After all, She was one of us: She lived and died a woman. And yet She had the courage and openness of heart to say "yes" to the greatest opportunity imaginable. By consenting to God's request of Her, She became "the first of the believers in the New Covenant." [1]

Mary is a complex figure who upholds several spiritual ideals at once. As the *theotokos*, or godbearer, She shows us that there is no limit to what we can do in this world if we are willing to enter fully into a covenant with the Divine. As a mother, She conveys a warmth and a compassion to those of us who might otherwise feel cut off from the direct experience of God's love. And, as one whose faith was sorely tried by watching Her own Son's cruel death, the Holy Mother understands the difficulty of keeping faith. She knows the importance of tangible confirmation in a world where one's dreams can too easily come to a tragic end. She was, Herself, blessed with such proof when Her Son returned from the dead. Indeed, according to tradition, Jesus went first to Her after the Resurrection to show Her — His beloved Mother — that Her faith had not been in vain.

And so, we should not be surprised that Mary wants the same for us.

The Holy Mother has been working since the very beginning to bring God's grace and mercy into our physical experience. In the early years of the Christian era, She began manifesting to individuals in the context of their prayer and devotional lives. She presented

Herself from the beginning as "only" a messenger or a mediator of God's will. In the third century, for instance, Mary and the apostle John appeared to a monk, St. Gregory the Wonderworker. As Gregory beheld them in a blaze of white light, he heard Mary tell John to teach him "the secret of the true faith," which John did.

Since 1000 A.D, when the Church began keeping records of such experiences, Mary has appeared over 21,000 times.[2] At first, most of the recipients of these visions were monks, nuns, and well-known spiritual figures within the Church — such as St. Teresa of Avila and St. Ignatius of Loyola. The Church treated their visions as an inspiring byproduct of a sanctified life, but did not consider them a communication to the world in general.

The first "modern" apparition of the Holy Mother took place outside Mexico City, ten years after the Spanish conquest. In 1531 A.D, Mary appeared to a newly converted Aztec Indian, Juan Diego, as he was walking to Mexico City to receive Christian instruction. There on the barren hillside where they stood, She introduced herself as the Virgin Mary, told him that She wanted a church built there so pilgrims could come there and worship. Juan immediately took this message to the bishop and was turned away for obvious reasons. On his way back, Juan encountered Mary again. She convinced him to go back and try again the next day. Even though Juan could not figure out why She had chosen him, a lowly peasant, he agreed to try once more.

Impressed with his sincerity, the bishop told Juan that he needed some proof that he wasn't making it all up. When Juan went back and told Mary what the bishop had said, She asked him to return the following day to receive the proof that the bishop requested. But the next day, Juan's uncle became terribly ill, and so he went in search of help for his ailing uncle. Hoping that the Lady would forgive him for missing the appointment, he took a path around the mountain to avoid Her. But Mary stood in his way, as She had other plans for him. After assuring him that his uncle would be okay, Mary told Juan to go pick some of the dew-covered roses that were miraculously growing on the mountain top in the mid-winter cold. When he returned to the path below, he found Mary waiting. She then helped him arrange the roses inside his crude overcoat, or *tilma*, and sent him into Mexico city to visit the bishop, once again.

When Juan spread his *tilma* and the roses at the feet of the bishop and a visitor — who just so happened to be the new governor of Mexico — they witnessed an even greater miracle than fresh roses in winter. On the inside of his garment, they beheld a beautiful painting that depicted the Holy Mother in prayer. They fell to their knees before Her image and were convinced, finally, that our Lady had appeared to Juan. Her request was fulfilled, and a magnificent cathedral stands today on the spot where "Our Lady of Guadalupe" first appeared to him. It enshrines the unfaded original painting that Juan received over 450 years ago.

Given the subject matter of this book, it is significant that Mary saw fit to manifest Her image *in the form of a painting* to the people of Mexico. Since then, innumerable thinkers have concluded that Mexico's distinct religious and cultural identity can be traced to the vision — and the surviving image — of Our Lady of Guadalupe.

Over 300 years later, the era of European apparitions began in earnest and assumed the pattern set forth by the Mexico apparition. Mary began to reveal herself to ordinary people — mostly women and children — outside the walls of the Church and to disseminate messages clearly meant for a wider audience. From the beginning of this new phase, Mary's public messages have rarely evidenced anything new or surprising in terms of spiritual teachings. They have "merely" reiterated the importance of the enduring spiritual truths espoused by Jesus in the Gospels. The only "news" that She has brought to us — if it can be called that at all — concerns our collective future if we should fail to heed God's call: Serving as His messenger, She repeatedly admonishes us to begin living according to what we have been taught in the Scriptures, or *we will soon reap the consequences of our failure to do so.*

Essentially, She invites us to do what She did — to say "yes" to God — and to submit to the requirements of a fully spiritualized life. Along these lines, when Lucia, the principal visionary at Fatima, was asked what was the main message of Mary at Fatima, she replied, "The main request of our Lady is that we offer up each day whatever God requests of us."[3] We have now been told in several successive apparitions that if we can do this "simple" thing, then we can avert the upheavals that must otherwise ensue from our neglect of God's will.

At first, Mary appeared only to Catholics. But more recently, visions and locutions (i.e. an inner voice) of Mary have been reported by non-Catholics, as well. Her messages seem increasingly universal in scope, and the ways in which She manifests seem less tied to traditional Catholic beliefs and dogmas. As Father Faricy has said, "In each of Her comings, Mary appears in such a way that the people to whom She comes can relate to Her. To black people She is black. To Koreans, She looks Korean ... She comes as their Mother, and that is what She is. Ours, too."[4] Not only does She appear in the forms culturally and religiously tailored to the visionaries, but Her messages convey an increasingly universal tone. Indeed, She has specifically said to the visionaries in

Medjugorje that She is *the mother of all nations*. And, when Mary first came to Annie Kirkwood, Annie told Mary that She had the wrong person because she (Annie) was not a Catholic. Mary replied, "Nor am I."[5]

The Holy Mother clearly intends to break free from the forms that have previously bound Her and to advocate for the needs of humanity as a whole.

In addition to conveying a more ecumenical message — even to the extent of communicating through non-Catholic visionaries — Mary's presence is increasingly associated with physical miracles and tangible, phenomenal manifestations. Of course, Mary's association with miracles and other "prodigies" is not new. This role can be traced back to the Gospel account of the wedding at Cana,[6] where She urged Jesus to perform His first public miracle against His own initial inclination. Confident that He would consent to Her request, She told the servants, "Whatever He saith unto you, do it." The simple authority in these words have convinced Christians that She, indeed, knows Her Son's heart and will better than anyone else. Over the centuries, not surprisingly, She has come to represent the motherly force that gently ushers God's love "downward" until it reveals itself in a myriad of forms — from stunning supernatural displays to simple, heartfelt miracles that speak to us where we live.

Consistent with this role, the Blessed Mother has manifested physical, miraculous phenomena at virtually every major apparition that onlookers could see, if only briefly. For instance, in 1917 at Fatima, tens of thousands witnessed a spectacular transformation of the sun that could be seen many miles away. And, in the early 60s, onlookers at Garabandal, Spain, witnessed a "little miracle" when a communion host wafer briefly appeared on Conchita's tongue as Mary administered communion to her. Most recently, in Medjugorje, thousands of pilgrims continue to witness transformations of the sun reminiscent of Fatima, crosses of light in the clouds, and other radiant phenomena associated with the Holy Mother's apparitions.

Almost without exception, each successive major apparition has appeared to more visionaries, lasted longer, and spawned more miraculous phenomena than those that have preceded them. This trend is heading, it seems, in the direction of something permanent. Mary herself has supported this expectation: She has promised at Garabandal and Medjugorje that greater miracles will follow — phenomena that will leave a *permanent visual sign that all the world can see.*

One such "miracle" may have already occurred in the privacy of one woman's spiritual relationship with the Holy Mother.

When I first learned of Michele Livingston's encounters with Mary and the angels — and the commission she received to create paintings of the Holy Mother's essence — I realized that this could be the next step in Mary's manifestation to the world. Given Mary's outreach to non-Catholics, Michele's open-minded belief system seemed to provide a doorway to the world as a whole. Also, given Michele's artistic training and spiritual responsiveness, it made sense that the Holy Mother — who was Herself chosen to conceive a new birth — might not perform a miracle out of "whole cloth," but would elect to work through another handmaiden to co-create a miracle that others could thereafter contemplate.

Regardless, Michele's visionary paintings and lessons clearly represent *the first enduring, multidimensional expression of Mary's message to the world.* Indeed, the Holy Mother has now

xxx

manifested — through the willingness of a modern artist and mystic — a permanent creation that works through the dual channels of verbal and visual communication to produce its effect on the beholder.

Now there are those who will try to make a new gospel of this work by accepting every word and every image with unquestioned belief. And, there are those who will reject the whole on the basis of some real or imagined theological error. I urge you to do neither, and to accept that the truth always lies somewhere in between — on that sacred ground where divine *intention* and human *responsiveness* mingle to produce *revelation.* From this standpoint, we can accept that the Holy Mother's spirit infused every word and every brushstroke without insisting that this work sprang fully formed from the heavenly realms. While we might not like to admit it, any spiritual channel — no matter how pure — must ultimately render whatever she receives into a form that we can readily understand. She must draw upon her own vocabulary and her own beliefs to express the wordless impulse that anoints her in the moment of deep communion. Through this co-creative process, she influences what she receives, yes; but in the end, while the creation may fall short of perfection, the Divine appears to us as *personal* and *real.* What greater miracle can there be?

This morning, during my hour of meditation and prayer, I prayed that the Holy Mother would guide me as I wrote these words about Michele's beautiful book. Before long, a familiar, gentle energy "descended" upon me, and I found myself energized and overshadowed by Her presence. Then I heard the words, *"We are here."*

For those who have opened their hearts, Mary and Jesus are truly and simply here. But, while we might believe this to be "spiritually" true, most of us still react with surprise when they manifest personally and tangibly to us for the first time. It is so easy to feel unworthy, if not downright scared, and to wonder what we could have possibly done — right or wrong — to deserve their presence. We may even try to talk them out of it! Indeed, I am reminded of a woman who saw Jesus appear at a prayer meeting. He walked among the group with such love in His eyes, but only she could see Him. The woman asked Him, "Why me? There are people here who are far more worthy to see You than I am." Jesus replied, "Why *not* you?"[7]

If we could feel the truth of these words for ourselves, the implications would be staggering. For, Jesus didn't list the reasons that the woman deserved to see Him. Instead, He implied that *nothing* could render her *un*worthy in His eyes. What love!

If Jesus and the Holy Mother find us unconditionally acceptable, too — and are willing to be seen by us — then why do so few of us experience Them directly? Even if They accept us unconditionally, for some reason most of us remain closed to Them, insensitive to Their touch and blind to Their presence. Apparently the problem is ours. So what stands in the way?

When Mary first appeared to Michele, she reacted as most of us would have. Like Annie Kirkwood, she questioned Mary's choice of her as a channel. After all, Michele was not a Catholic, nor did she have a previous relationship with the Holy Mother. It seemed to come out of nowhere

Mary told Michele that she possessed a quality that accounted for Mary's ability to work through her. It was not because Michele had amassed great knowledge or wisdom or power. It was because she possessed the one thing upon which the Divine can establish a relationship with a human being — an obedient, childlike spirit.

When I first met Michele, I could appreciate why Mary would choose this woman, for Michele radiates an infectious joy and good humor. When I think of Michele, I think of her laughing. Though she is sophisticated and worldly-wise, she nonetheless exhibits a brightness and a simple faith in which the Holy Mother apparently takes great pleasure.

It seems like such a simple thing to manifest a childlike and obedient spirit. But most of us have "put on" so many layers of complexity that the spiritual path becomes for us not so much a process of acquiring anything new, but of relinquishing what we never needed. In view of this, what we know and refuse to relinquish may impede our spiritual sensitivity and greater development just as effectively as any real or imagined sinfulness. Of all the great beings who have emerged in the Western spiritual tradition, Mary rises above all the rest in exemplifying a childlike openness of mind and heart. From the time that She replied to the angel, *Let it be done to me according to what you say,* She has served as the best example of someone who completely submitted to God's calling. Further, She was courageous enough to give "uninformed consent" — that is, She said "yes" without really knowing what lay before her.

Through Michele's paintings and the lessons that she has received from the Holy Mother and the angelic forces, we have an unprecedented opportunity to feel divine presence in our lives through a modern artist and mystic who said "yes" to God's request. But we, too, must give our uninformed consent. We must leave the critical mind at the door not knowing what we may find, and enter into this spiritual work with a childlike, affirming spirit. Otherwise, we may stumble unnecessarily over particular words, or elements of individual artistic style. If we succumb to cynicism, the mind will reign victorious, but the heart will lose its tenuous hold, and we will remain bereft of what we truly need.

But if we can let go, then we may enter into that sacred realm of the heart where the Holy Mother found Michele waiting and willing. And then we, too, will possess the open-hearted quality most sought by those who seek to bring greater love into this world.

G. Scott Sparrow, Ed.D.
I Am with You Always: True Stories of Encounters with Jesus (Bantam, 1995), and *Blessed Among Women: Encounters with Mary and Her Message* (Harmony, 1998), and *The Perfect Gift* (Blue Mantle, 1998)

M.A. Livingston

The Annunciation

Mary's Message

*The gentle announcing of what the
Lord has for all of you is the rebirthing of
our souls. As Gabriel appeared to me because
I was humble and contrite of heart, so shall the
Love of God come upon you and announce your
rebirthing. As I gave birth to the Savior of our
souls, so shall you give birth to hope among
nations and hope for the raising of
our soul consciousness.*

Description of Painting

The concept of the first painting centers on the Annunciation, when the angel Gabriel appears to Mary, announcing that She is to be the Mother of God. Annunciation means to announce. We need to listen with our hearts and spirits to "news" of Higher Awareness not only in our daily meditation, but also throughout the day on a moment by moment basis.

According to Rev. Nerius Semmler in the *Emblems of Excellence*, "The lily represents purity of heart and has long been associated with the event of the Annunciation. This flower is spotlessly white, beautiful in form, and sweet in fragrance—a fitting flower for a holy, pure, and sinless soul."[1] Also in the painting are diagonal strokes leading up to Mary's face. They symbolize a staircase to Higher Awareness — *our oneness with God*. The three rays of light above Her head mean the same.

Background
Luke 1:26-28

In the sixth month the angel Gabriel was sent from God to the city of Nazareth in Galilee, to a virgin betrothed to a man whose name was Joseph, of the house of David, and the virgin's name was Mary. And he came to her and said, "Hail, O favored one, the Lord is with you!" But She was greatly troubled at the saying, and considered in Her mind what sort of greeting this might be. And the angel said to Her, "Do not be afraid, Mary, for you have found favor in God. And behold, you will conceive in your womb and bear a Son, and you shall call His name Jesus."

Mary said to the angel, "How can this be, since I have no husband?" The angel said to Her, "The Holy Spirit will come upon you, and the power of the Most High will overshadow you; therefore, the child to be born will be called holy, the Son of God."

Mary responded, "Behold, I am the handmaid of the Lord; let it be done to me according to your word."

Mary's Lesson

The painting, "The Annunciation," represents *humility*. All need to remain humble before the throne of our Creator. From our Lord you have come and from our Lord you shall return.

Love is the key. Humility and patience bind love together. When you love, you need to think of doing it in a humble, compassionate, and unselfish way. When you receive spiritual gifts, you need to remember that they come from our Creator, that all are here to do His will, that all are here to serve Him.

Remember when you look into people's faces, into their eyes, they are also children of God. Treat them with respect. Remain humble in your daily walk. Praise the Lord daily. Give Him thanks and gratitude. It is He who has created your soul, and unto His bosom you shall return. The humble come into God's arms first.

Many *gifts of the spirit* are given and many are called — few are chosen. The Lord in His infinite wisdom is able to disseminate His gifts in the ways He feels necessary. Spiritual gifts come in many forms.

The *gift of prophecy* means that one is able to proclaim the word of God, to align with the creative thought patterns of our Creator, and to remain humble in His works, to remain humble in this gift. Prophecy is for the upliftment of humanity, for encouragement, and for good counsel.

The *gift of discernment* provides you with the knowing of what is for your highest good. Your highest good is to do our Creator's will, our Father's will. When you align with the power of our Heavenly Father, you truly will receive all the gifts of the spirit. Discernment is knowing what is right for you. You need to pray for the gift of discernment. You will find as you gain discernment, and as you evolve in your spiritual knowing of God, and in your spiritual journey, discernment will be a part of you. You will be drawn into the things that are of the Lord. You will be drawn into that which is for your highest good.

The Lord plants a knowing within our hearts, so that what feels right and feels good for us in our prayer time, in our meditation time, is from the Lord. If it gives you peace, it's from the Lord. If it banishes confusion and implants within you a sense of security and stability, it's from the Lord. If it brings you joy and happiness, it's from the Lord. Discernment means knowing what is from the Lord and what is not.

Remember, the key is love. Please, my dear children, remain humble in love, for love boasts not. Love does not conquer. Love is gentle, and love is kind. Strive for humility, not to lower oneself, not to be less than your fellow man, but to know that you were created in love, that God is all powerful, all knowing, omnipresent, and omnipotent. He flows through you. He is in every creation. When anything is created, *God is there*!

To remain humble, I suggest that you walk in nature. Look at the wondrous and beautiful creation around you. Cycles come and cycles go. Things change, things evolve, but God is constant. He is constant in His love for humanity, and He is constant in His love for you as an individual. God never ceases loving His creation. True humility comes from an upright heart.

There are many gifts of the spirit. Read the Bible and you will understand them all. If a gift uplifts humanity, again, if it encourages, if it guides, if it directs for the good, then it is a true gift of the spirit.

Humility is a gift of the spirit. There are references to humility in the Bible. My Son, the Christ, remained humble even to the very end. When He said "Father, forgive them, for they know not what they do," He meant:

Father, I come from You, I am Your Son, You have created me. I put You first, dear Lord. I put You first in my heart, in my mind and my soul. Whatever happens around me externally, I need to release insofar as I am here to serve You, Lord. I am here to serve You first. I am here also to serve others and to love myself. If I have been rebuked and chided and misunderstood, only You, Lord, know the heart of the man. Only You can test the heart of the man.

So when Christ said, "Forgive them for they know not what they do," He was *being* in a state of humility.

Each one on this earth plane has a mission. The Lord created your soul, your body, your mind, your essence. Your soul is eternal. Your soul is indestructible. Your soul is a beam of light from the Creator's heart. I want you, dear children, all of you, to remember we are all beams of light. We are many rays. There is nothing but light in the heavenly realms, beautiful light. One needs to temper oneself on a daily basis, and to take a spiritual accounting of the progression of each day — not to judge oneself or be harsh on oneself — but knowing that progress is good, and it is being called for in each and every one of you.

As we evolve and move closer to the heart of God, the love of God, we grow in humility. Humility walks softly. Humility shows compassion. Humility bends an ear and listens. Humility, again, judges not. Humility is long-standing. Try, my children, to put humility into your hearts. Try to remain humble, knowing that you are from the Creator, you are from the Lord, and you are all here on a mission. Pray that you find your mission. Remember, you are part of the whole. A rose has many petals, but there is one stem that supports it.

This painting, "The Annunciation," means humility. When Gabriel appeared to me, I bowed my head. I remained humble. I knew that my mission was a higher mission, and it was filled with great love and honor. I did question the angel as to why me? Gabriel said:

Blessed among women you are. I am the messenger
sent by God to announce the good news. You are
chosen, Mary, because of your humble heart. You
are chosen, Mary, because of your ability to accept
the Holy Call. As you come from the Creator, the
Creator knows every cell of your body, knows
every thought before you think it. You have
remained pure, and you are chosen.

On a daily basis, I, Mary, remained humble. I showed compassion for my people. I showed love for humanity. I am the Mother of all of you. Come to me in trust, and I will intercede for you. I will take your prayers to Heaven. One does not gain humility. One does not search for it. It starts within the heart. To foster humility within your heart:

1. Do a kindness or a good deed for a stranger, someone that you do not know, and someone that will possibly not find out who bestowed the kindness or the good deed. This is humility.

2. In prayer time, get down on your knees if you can — by your bedside or wherever you feel comfortable — and ask the Lord to show you true humility, and our Creator will show you humility. Feel the love when you kneel to pray. Feel God's blessings come upon you. Humility remains grateful. Humility remains in a state of thankfulness.

3. Be gentle with yourselves. God knows your accomplishments as he knows your thoughts. Do not worry about what man thinks of you. Think about how your Creator abides within you.

Humility does come in many different forms. It comes when we least expect it. Flattery or compliments sometimes tend to deceive, depending on how they are given. We have observed that the earth plane at times falls into the deception of flattery. Love yourselves — you are children of God. Do not be deceived by flattery. Remain strong in your convictions. Remain in a state of love and honor. Respect yourselves as you respect others, as you respect your Divine Creator. Count humility as a gift; count it as a blessing.

I honor you, my dear children, and I love you. Remember, you are equal in God's eyes — all of you. Be kind to one another and to yourselves. Be gentle. God's love knows no bounds.

Your accomplishments in God's eyes are different than your accomplishments in man's eyes. Many on the earth plane get caught up in pleasing man. There is nothing wrong with pleasing your fellow man, but remember, God loves you unconditionally. Serve your Lord. Ask Him His will for your life. Ask Him what He would have you do. The answers will come to you.

Sometimes when you are humble, you don't perceive yourselves to be, for true humility is being in a state of grace. Sometimes true humility does not perceive itself as such. But I tell you, as I send all of you love, that one of the main keys to accepting your call is humility. And so, when you gaze upon the painting, "The Annunciation" — the soft blues and greens, the white lily of purity — *remember humility.*

God's peace be with you. His blessings be upon you.

Meditation

I have come here now, in this age, more than ever before to announce good tidings. The world has come into a time of rebirthing. Prayers are rising to the heavens — they are received and heard. See in every face, in every leaf in nature, in every rose — the Creator! You are from one eternal God. You have been forgiven, saved, and redeemed. All you must do is ask. It is not too late to call upon the

Lord. As Gabriel announced the news of great joy to me, I was obedient to the Lord. Our Heavenly Father requests obedience. Do unto others as you would have them do unto you. Forgive others. Use the white lily of purity that Gabriel handed me to cleanse all pain away. Sometimes you bring pain upon yourselves by your anger and fear. You are here to have life and have it more abundantly.

Calm your mind. Sit quietly and take a few deep breaths. Close your eyes. Visualize a white lily. It is being handed to you by the archangel Gabriel, who is kneeling in front of you now. Hold the lily, and as its petals unfold to you, so shall all that is divine and cleansing be yours. Smell its sweet fragrance. I ask that you accept this white lily in honor of obedience. Now, hold the thought of its purity in your mind — meditate for a few minutes upon its meaning for you — and then place it in your heart. You are loved, dear children, just as you are. God's grace be upon all of you.

The Annunciation Prayer

Dear Heavenly Father whose love knows no bounds,

be with us this day and always.

Be with us as we open our hearts to announce our truth.

Our truth and Your truth is Your word,

O Most Holy Father.

Let Your word remain in our hearts for the days ahead.

When we are tossed and turned by the distractions of this world,

help us to know that Your word is forever alive.

We all were conceived in love.

Our life is the gift of Your love.

You are pure love — our Creator!

We pray for Your will for each and every life.

We pray for love to shine for all mankind.

We pray for courage to announce what is true.

Please, most gracious Father, send Your angels to protect us

and Your powerful love to surround us.

We ask this in Your name.

Amen.

Archangel Gabriel Speaks on "The Annunciation"

I oversee painting number one, "The Annunciation," for I am the great messenger. I have been portrayed in many paintings throughout the centuries kneeling in front of Mary and handing Her a white lily.

Each archangel vibrates with certain tasks. As the great messenger or the angel of revelation, I deliver things to people. I've been on hand at many good events and delivered much good news.

At the Annunciation, the Creator wanted more of a gentle archangel to approach Mary so that She would fear not. I appeared to Her then as a tall androgynous-looking figure, with a long, white robe, bare feet, and white fluffy wings; but I emanated that golden pure light, with more of a female, vibrational essence.

It was a beautiful sunny afternoon when I was ordered to approach our Lady. She was quite delicate in appearance and very, very childlike, for at the time She was around the age of fourteen. She was alone and on Her knees, scrubbing the floor. I entered through the side of the wall with pure, white, blinding light. Mary dropped what She was doing. I said to Her:

> *Hark, Mary I am Gabriel the great messenger. I am here to announce good tidings which will bring humanity great joy. For You are chosen, Mary. You are chosen to be the Mother of God, the Mother of our Savior who will bring humanity great joy.*

Mary looked very stunned. Her mouth fell open, She did not speak a word. For She was overcome with great awe, and I said,

> *Hail Mary, this is true. You have been chosen for blessed are You among women. You have been chosen*

for Your humility, for Your divine grace, and for
Your obedience to accept the Holy Call.

Mary then bowed Her head. She did not believe at first the words that were given unto Her, but through the power of our Heavenly Creator, Her heart was opened and love poured forth like liquid gold. It was not the first time that Mary and I had conversations. It is only this one that is recorded in the Bible. I announced different events to Her throughout Her lifetime.

"The Annunciation" is symbolic of humility. It is a very beautiful painting, a very delicate painting. Remember the faces in the paintings are not necessarily Mary's physical face, but they personify the gentle, feminine, divine essence of the world — the Mother love which is Mary. This delicate face is looking upon the white lily. The white lily represents again purity. White is the color of cleansing. Mary was not only pure of heart, She was also a virgin, and She was Herself immaculately conceived. The Mother of God was preordained to be immaculately conceived as the Christ was immaculately conceived.

The lily also represents truth. Mary is gazing upon the lily for it brings not only truth to Her heart, the Holy Call, but also the truth of Christ.

For Christ said unto the world, "I am the way, the truth, and the life. Come unto me and I shall set you free."

The lily is a powerful meditation symbol. It denotes releasing anything that is unlike God — all negativity — emotional and mental baggage that you carry on your back. Gaze upon the lily in your heart. Visualize it in your mind. Remember it.

The tones in this painting are also very cleansing, very healing. You, as human beings on the earth plane, are like walking prisms of light. White is at the top of the head or the crown of the head.

Purple is the highest spiritual color that goes across the forehead, which is the seat of intuition. Royal or indigo blue is at the lower face region. Turquoise is at the throat, and emerald green is at the heart region. This painting mainly vibrates with the colors from the heart region on up. It has a lot of very soothing shades of blue, green, and purple. Therefore, it will announce the truth to you because it is a painting of healing. As human beings, you need to walk your truth, speak your truth, and live your truth. For all can be messengers, one to the other, of God's word.

You may call upon me, archangel Gabriel, in any speaking engagements that you might be giving. For I am the almighty messenger, and I will help you speak the truth if you are fearful in front of people. I will help you, and give you courage to say what is right and to say what is true. I am not only the messenger of truth, but I am the angel of resurrection, of revelation. I guard over all of Heaven, and I deliver and interpret visions.

When you look and gaze upon the painting, "The Annunciation," think of being healed in areas where you try to remain in control in your life. Many of you hold back your own truth — your own true identity. You do not communicate with your spouse, your friends, or neighbors. You feel that by trying to hold back or trying to keep control in your life that you will be safe. But you all need to communicate, unite, and share, one to another. You need to announce how you feel, not to hurt another on the earth plane, but to share your truth.

Annunciation, of course, means to announce or to make a proclamation. So I shall, as Gabriel, proclaim to you, *be your own person!* You need to announce your own truth, to do what you feel you need to do. Do you believe in God? Do you believe in Jesus Christ who died for you? Do you believe that Mary is the Mother of our divine Savior? Do you believe that Mary loves you? To help you with the energy shift and with the consciousness shift from the earth plane to the fourth dimension, you need to speak your truth in the way of gentleness, kindness, and deliberation.

This painting also represents new beginnings and the ability to purify, cleanse, and clear out the old — to make room for the new to enter your lives. It is time now to detox the body of chemicals, by drinking distilled water. Take an inventory — a physical, mental, and spiritual inventory. Release what is no longer for your highest good. It is time now to cleanse the earth plane. To assist you in this cleansing process, say also a mighty prayer — the prayer of discernment:

> *Please dear Lord, let me release anything that is no longer for my highest good. Let me attract those into my energy space that are for my highest good, and release those who are not. Let me attract situations that are for my highest good, and let me release those situations that are not for my highest good. May I speak my truth to the world.*
>
> *Amen.*

Discernment is a knowing of what's right for you. It is time now to take a stand for the messenger of the truth. What is your truth? This does not mean you need to join the ministry. It does not mean that you have to give up everything you have. But on your daily walk give a smile, give truth to somebody. By doing so know that you bring truth back to yourself.

So again, take an accounting; take a mental, physical, and spiritual inventory, of where you have been and what you need to release. Those things that you need to release are no longer for your highest good, so release them and let them go.

I am here to announce to you that you are a child of the living God. I am here to say that each one of you on the earth plane also has a Holy Call. Whatever that mission is, you need to find it within your own heart. Whatever brings you joy and brings joy to others is your true mission — your *soul's purpose*. Each and every one of you on the earth plane has a true soul's purpose that God has instilled within you.

Our blessed and dear Mother Teresa of Calcutta walked her truth. She loved the people of India and the people of the world. She found love in every human heart, and she gave out love to every human being. She loved what she was doing; therefore, she was fulfilling her true mission. You cannot all do what Mother Teresa did, nor are all of you possibly inclined to do what she did. But finding your own truth means finding what you love to do and doing it with all your might, doing it with all your heart. So whether you are a good gardener, or cook, or seamstress, or conversationalist, or nurturer, or motivator — whatever you love to do — do it with all your heart and might for this is your truth. This is what we call in the heavenly realms, walking your truth, talking your truth, being the divine co-creator that you are.

The number one represents the Holy Divine — one in all and all in one. One represents the beginning; therefore "The Annunciation" represents the beginning of our Savior's life, and thus it was placed in the first position of the twelve paintings.

The Mystical Rose

Mary's Message

As love poured from my heart and
opened like an eternal rose, with fragrance of
love exuding, so shall love for humanity pour
from your hearts as you open up to your Higher
Power. The Power within is my Son's — the
Christ Consciousness, one of pure love.

Description of Painting

The *Mystical Rose* is an age-old symbol of the Blessed Mother, and one of Her titles. The large rose in the second painting signifies Mary's love for God, which is exhaled like an exquisite perfume from Her heart. It is also a symbol of the most pure, immaculate heart of Her and the love She also bears for us, Her children.

Within this rose there is a triangle with an eye-shape in the center, which represents the Blessed Trinity. "As three sides form one triangle, so the three divine persons of the Trinity are equal to but distinct from one another — one God. The eye denotes the all-seeing omnipresent God."[3]

The dashed "M" initial under the rose stands for Mary and also miracle. In the background are three pyramids (triangular shapes) which are power symbols of our own unlimited, divine, God-within power.

Background

Although there is no biblical reference to Mary as the *Mystical Rose*, in the words of Cardinal John Newman, "Mary is the most beautiful flower ever seen in the spiritual world. It is by the power of God's grace that from the barren earth there ever sprung up at all flowers of holiness and glory: and Mary is the Queen of them. She is the Queen of spiritual flowers; and therefore, is called the Rose, for the rose is the most beautiful. She is the Mystical or Hidden Rose, for mystical means hidden."[3]

Mary's Lesson

The painting, "The Mystical Rose," represents *unconditional love.* Love is like a body of water. It is like the ocean, with many fingers, with many tributaries, with many rivers, with many streams. Love never ends. Love is eternal. God is love.

Unconditional love means, of course, love that has no bounds, loving regardless of, loving in a state of constancy. Pure unconditional love flows from the heart like living waters.

All in this world were created from the thought forms of God. He conceived you from His holy heart. He watches, He protects, He provides. His love is constant, is steady, is unswerving. Again, the love of God knows no bounds. God does not put a condition on His love. He loves all equally, and asks you to come to Him.

My Son, the Christ, loved His Heavenly Father unconditionally. He gave His life for His Holy Mission, for His Call. He gave His life to save you, to bring you back to the fold of grace. He loved unconditionally with a sensitivity, grace, and compassion that at times pierced His own heart, for the pangs of love were so great.

I ask you, all of you, to walk the path of my Son, the Christ. In your daily walk, moment by moment, try my children to remain in that state of grace and unconditional love. Again, judge not. Be long-suffering. Be patient with yourselves.

They have called me the *Mystical Rose*. A rose, indeed, is a thing of beauty. It is exquisitely perfect in every way. It starts as a bud, and petal by petal opens to show us, in all its glory, that it is a creation of God. Rose pink is a gentle color. It is the color of the heart. It is the color of unconditional love. Think of the beautiful shade of rose pink. Think of its healing abilities. Think of that color when you pray, when you pray for unconditional love to be in your heart — for yourself, for your fellow man, and for your Creator.

At times, my own heart opens so wide and exudes such unconditional love for my children that I want to give you roses; I want to share the fragrance of love in my heart for you. I count you more precious than anything. Each one of you is a petal of the rose of unconditional love.

I ask of you to open your hearts. Try to love your neighbors unconditionally. It is easy at times to love our children unconditionally, or even our pets. They give us back so much. It is most difficult at times to love our enemies unconditionally, to love the people that have hurt us. But forgiveness is the key to unconditional love; it is the purity of unconditional love.

To remain in a state of love and to be able to exude it as the fragrance of roses, I suggest that you enter into a state of forgiveness. In your human state, you have suffered many abuses and sometimes great pain — physical, emotional, and mental. Again to be in a state of pure unconditional love, you need to forgive.

I ask of you now to think of each individual who has hurt you. See their face in your mind's eye, and surround their face with pure, white light. Tell them that you love them, that you forgive them, that we are all children of God, that we are all God's equals.

By doing this, you release unconditional love — for it is boundless. As you give it, it grows and grows and grows. One bud opens, and when you give unconditional love, love blooms in all the gardens of your hearts in profusion.

This painting, "The Mystical Rose," is a powerful one. You were created in God's unconditional love. So every thought, every word, every deed, every purpose that you have innately within you is to share that love — to remain in it, to have it flow through you, to give it, and to keep on giving it.

Unconditional love produces peace within your hearts. It produces patience within your hearts, and of course, it produces humility — for virtues do tend to overlap.

Please be aware of your actions toward your fellow man. Remember, too, that it is most important as you give out unconditional love to humanity, that you bring it also back unto yourselves. Be gentle, be kind, be patient with yourselves.

Unconditional love is something that you don't really need to work on, but you need to ask to be shown how to love more. Many people feel that giving is synonymous with love, but giving is a by-product of unconditional love. True unconditional love has peace unto itself.

You can send unconditional love to the world through your prayer time. You can send it to your loved ones by your thoughts. You do not have to be in their presence. You do not have to *give* to show unconditional love. You just need *to be* and to send it; it will be received.

Think of love unconditionally pouring from your heart like liquid gold. Envision it pouring from your heart like fingers, like rivers of light, and touching each heart on this earth plane. You are all bound as one.

The tree has many branches. The tree, of course, is the root. The tree is the pillar of God. Tend your trees wisely, give them the nourishment they need so that the branches grow, extend, and touch others' lives.

You are part of the all. Unconditional love means unity. It is not a state of separateness. It is a state of wholeness, of oneness. It is also a state of completion, because unconditional love completes a circle. As we give it flows back. Remember, there are many different ways to give. It is fine to give financially to the church of God. It is fine to give to the poor. It is fine to give your time, energies, and support to the higher cause. True unconditional love is in a state of giving, but also receiving, so the circle is complete.

Take the *mystical rose* of unconditional love that I give you, my children. Hold it close; put it within your hearts.

I come to you now in a time of great turmoil. I know many of you are anxious for signs and wonders. But know that you are divinely loved and that God's way is sometimes higher than our way, as God's thoughts are higher than our own.

I come to you from the Father, from the Holy Father, the Heavenly Father of Lights. And I come with my Son, the Christ, because you are getting closer now to many earth changes. You must remember that although these earth changes come and many cry out in anguish, do not lose hope — please do not lose hope. Stay in your prayer time, love unconditionally, give God your all.

Sometimes it is difficult to think about — to acknowledge, to understand — being in a state of pure unconditional love, in a state of grace: But remember to try. *Please try!*

Once you are aware of your spiritual journey, and once you are aware that each thought you think ennobles and uplifts humanity, as do good deeds, then love is here within you. As you are aware of all these things and you try to reach closer to our Creator, then love is here within you — as it always has been. You are in a state of love when you try to meet with its total completion.

I love you, my people, my children. I open my mantle, and I pull you into me, into my heart, into my fold of love and grace. I am Mother of all of you. Remember, you are loved totally *unconditionally* by your Heavenly Father, now and forever more!

Meditation

Roses are my favorite flowers. They are beautiful and gentle. The great "unfolding" of what is to come, like the rose, will be revealed to you. You are now unfolding into a new time, a new dimension, a new realism. In preparation of my Son's, the Christ's, return, open your hearts. Let the pink light of unconditional love fill you and overflow through you. My heart opens for you with love. Be open to the scent of roses in the air. I love to leave my trace for humanity. Petal by petal unfolding, day by day, we climb ever closer to glory.

Do not be hard with yourselves, children; but be tender, like the petals of the rose. The rose is a mystical symbol for this time. This is an age of new awareness — of signs and wonders. Look to what is beyond your everyday existence. You are in the world and among the world, but I tell you, there will be an ascension for all who come to know me, my Son, and our Father. I long to be in your hearts. Remain open, dear ones, for what is to come. There are many earth changes coming — famine and pestilence. You are not being tested; you are being tempered and strengthened.

Take a few deep breaths and center your mind. Slowly close your eyes. Visualize being surrounded by a cocoon of rose pink light. How does that beautiful light feel to you? This is the light of unconditional love. Now, think of a large yet delicate rose of unconditional love. What color is your rose? It is the extension of the love you feel for yourself. See its every petal slowly unfolding to you. Gaze at the center of the rose. What do you see at the very center? What is at the center of the rose is perfect for you. Now receive it and feel the love that is yours.

The Mystical Rose Prayer

Dear Father in Heaven,

Open our hearts to receive all the goodness

You have for us.

As we have given, let us learn also to receive.

Let us receive Your love

and the "gifts of Your spirit"

in greater ways than ever before.

Keep our hearts pure and turn us away from evil.

Let the mighty "Mystical Rose" of unconditional love

well up within us.

Let us see the world in a new divine way each day.

Let us know that true power is within;

that we are co-creators with Your divine essence.

Soften our hearts to forgive

and to see beauty in every living thing.

Raise our hopes, dreams, and ideals to the highest pinnacle of truth.

We ask all these things in love,

knowing that every good and perfect gift is from above.

Thank you, Father God.

Amen.

Archangel Raphael on "The Mystical Rose"

The beautiful painting, "The Mystical Rose," painting number two, represents unconditional love. The rose is quite a thing of beauty. It is also called the *Rosa Mystica*. Our Lady's heart vibrates with the gentle color of rose pink. Rose pink is a healing color, and She sends the healing light of Her heart to all of humanity.

There are many symbols in this painting. The crescent moon to the left of Her face is a white stroke that represents the feminine, divine energy, for the lunar moon vibrates with the feminine. There are two doves, one near our Lady's left eye and one to the right of Her face. Doves represent gentleness. They represent peace. When you have unconditional love in your hearts, you also have peace. I come with the gentle healing power of peace today. For my sandals have trod far and wide throughout this earth plane, and I have seen those with great faith and unconditional love in their hearts be healed. Remember, the dove also symbolizes the power of the Holy Spirit. The pair of doves also represents equality — one to the other, man to woman, woman to man, God to man, and man to God, Heaven to earth, and earth to Heaven. As above, so below.

In this portrayal of our Lady is a white beam of light. This represents the seat of your own intuition, your own awareness, your own divinity. The golden yellow sweep from the left side of our Lady's cheek on up is a diagonal and vibrant sweep of golden light. It represents divine thought, divine will, and divine power. Our Lady had divine will to precede with Her Call. She had divine power that was given to Her by the Holy Spirit. She also had divine love within Her heart. Her heart is like that of the *mystical rose*.

That is one of Her names or titles. It was bestowed upon Her many centuries ago around the time of the middle ages.

Roses themselves have a very gentle, healing property. They are quite a lovely flower and as each petal unfolds it gives the individual something new to ponder. In this painting, the rose is very powerful. It looks like it's rising above the seas of light. There is green in the lower portion emanating from the rose. I, Raphael, vibrate with the color green. Green is the ultimate color of healing. This rose of unconditional love is being pushed upward through the power of healing. Look at the rose and you will see its many petals unfolding before you. There is a heart-shaped petal within the rose itself, down at the very bottom. Again, this represents containment of heart love. Petal by petal the rose unfolds to you to show you God's creation in all its perfection.

The Trinity or the triangular shape is shown four times in this painting. There is a triangle contained in the rose at the very center. That represents the Holy Trinity, and the swirling eye shape within the triangle represents the all seeing eye of our Divine Creator — God. The triangles are power symbols to help you unlock the divine godhead within. There is also a row of three triangular or pyramidical shapes in the middle left section of the painting.

There is beautiful blue water at the bottom of this painting, and aqua colors that emanate from it. Water is very cleansing and very healing. I symbolically bring to you today a golden bowl of water. It has cleansing properties for humanity. There is water contained in many of these twelve paintings. Water reminds you to get in touch with your fluid soul-conscious mind — your soul-mind which communes with the Creator. I enjoy overseeing gardens where there are ponds, lakes, streams. Wherever there is water, I am also there.

I vibrate, above all else, with love. Again, love heals all. Love conquers all. Love melts the icy hearts of man. Love shines brighter than any sun or star. Love is the core of all that is. Let the flow of this painting enter within your soul, your mind, your heart. Let the love well up within you, pushing your own rose of love to the surface. Think of the gentle fragrance of the rose. Think of its soft delicate petals.

My energy, along with our Blessed Mother's, comes through the painting in every stroke, hue, tone, and color. This is a *point of contact* painting. As you view it, feel the healing flow of unconditional love emanating from it and flowing like liquid gold into your heart. Reach out and receive your healing, in the name of our Almighty God, and our ever-loving Christ. Remember to pray for healing in all areas of your life. Pray for others and their healing as well.

Love is the same in any language. It is the ultimate unspoken truth. Unconditional love also is synonymous with forgiveness, for to forgive is the most healing thing that one can do for one's self and for others. Because I love gardens and because there is healing love in gardens, I want to remind you of a saying: "Forgiveness is the fragrance the violet sheds on the heel that crushed it."

You have all been crushed. You have all been wounded, abused in some way, and abandoned at times. You have all felt lost and confused, for that is a human condition. But forgiveness turns the other cheek. Forgiveness is the ultimate healer.

So I commend you now, as archangel Raphael, to forgive those who have hurt you — to turn the other cheek so to speak. Think of those who have wronged you. In your mind, surround their face with pure white light, send them unconditional love, and release them. This is very, very important. For to be made whole in all areas of your life and to be healed in those areas, you must forgive. Forgiveness is the key to feeling unconditional love.

When you look at the painting, "The Mystical Rose," you will feel love welling up within you. Unconditional love has a tenderness, a gentleness, a peace, that surpasses all understanding. Accept this painting into your hearts and know that the healing energy of love stands behind it, as I stand behind it, in front of it, below it, above it, and beside it.

I come from one God Creator, and I was created again to oversee many things on this earth plane. I am quite joyous when I am assigned to couples who are in love. For anything that love touches also heals. There is a saying that love heals all wounds. This is true.

Blessings to all who read the words of our Lady. Understand their meaning and take them to heart, for She is the most beloved in the garden of Heaven. She is the most beautiful of all, because Her spirit shines forth with such love not only for Her Son, the Christ, but for each and every individual on the earth plane. Blessings on all those who hear these words and accept them, for you shall receive many, many healings in God's speed.

Number two is a dual number. It represents duality. It also represents coexistence. Two is a very balancing number. The painting, "The Mystical Rose," is the expression of loving all of creation — loving all of creation equally — man to woman, man to animal, man to Creator, and so on. This painting was placed in the second position, because you need to show unconditional love to others and also to bring it back unto yourselves.

The Nativity

Mary's Message

No greater love is there from a
mother to her child, or from the Creator
to His children. The circle of life continues
eternally, only in different stages. Be tender to
yourselves, to each other, and to your children.
God's grace knows no bounds. Peace be among you.
Unless you become as children, you cannot enter
the Kingdom of Heaven, my blessed ones.

Description of Painting

In "The Nativity" Mary is shown with Her baby — the Redeemer of the world. The baby Jesus here is symbolic of miracles, a new life, beginnings, and salvation.

The colors in this piece are the most vibrant and varied of the twelve paintings, denoting joy and hope for the future. We have a Savior! We are not alone! The star represents our ideals and dreams, which are ever possible with God and our beautiful inner child, who loves, guides, directs, and sets us free. The circular movement of color around the Madonna and Child signifies eternal love for humanity.

Background

Luke 2:4-7

And Joseph also went up from Galilee, from the city of Nazareth, to Judea, to the city of David, which is Bethlehem, because he was of the house and lineage of David, to be enrolled with Mary, his betrothed, who was with child. And while there the time came for Her to be delivered. And She gave birth to Her first-born son and wrapped Him in swaddling clothes, and laid Him in a manger, because there was no place for them in the inn.

Mary's Lesson

The painting, "The Nativity," represents *esteem of spiritual values*. Esteem means to consider, to think about, and that is what I want my children to do. I want them to consider, to regard, to think about spiritual values.

Spiritual values are unto themselves. One might think of them as gifts or virtues, but a value is something that is prized. A value is something that is regarded highly. Spiritual values belong to "The Nativity," because Christ — my Son, Jesus — came into this world to give us a code to live by — a moral code, a spiritual code, a soul, mind, and body code.

When I gave Him birth, it brought great joy to me as His mother and to the world. My Son, the Christ, brought a code of spiritual values for us to follow. Values are what God, our Creator, esteems most, because they are of God, they are one with God. We are all esteemed as individuals and regarded as valuable to God, as prized to God — every single one of us. Jesus was His Son in human form. You are also His sons and daughters in human form.

His Son, my Son the Christ in human form, taught us about spiritual values. Remember the meek. Remember the Beatitudes in the Bible. The Beatitudes are one of my Son's greatest teachings, for these are about spiritual values. The Beatitudes are synonymous with values. Read them and follow them.

Jesus came here to set an example for us to follow. I encourage you, all of you, to follow in His footsteps. Remember love. Remember the spiritual value of patience, forbearance, loving one another in all that is. Remember humility. Remember God's grace. Remember long-suffering. Remember the fruits of the spirit. We know if something is valuable; when it is valuable, it produces good fruits, good works.

My Son, the Christ, produced many good works. He healed many. He reached out His hand and He touched many. He did the work of His Father, our Father in Heaven. Please follow in my Son's footsteps, step-by-step each day. Be gentle with yourselves; love one another, be tender in heart and forgiving.

A baby is born. It brings great joy to the world. The angels smile in Heaven at each new birth, as do I, for the baby is a seed for the world. Through the child's growth and development, through his own flourishing, it gives us hope because each new child is a new hope.

You are in a time on the earth plane of birthing. Please, I ask of you, remain in your prayer time, for prayer can make the difference. Prayer can raise your consciousness towards our Creator. Remember to think good thoughts, pure thoughts, because thoughts are very powerful, as is prayer.

Please be aware that no prayer goes unheard or unanswered, and that every thought you have ever thought has either empowered humanity and yourself through love, or has broken down and weakened the link with all that is. It is a matter of being aware on a moment by moment or daily basis of our thoughts. Thoughts are more powerful than words. Thoughts and prayers almost become one. So remember, and think of your thoughts as prayers sent out. By doing this, you will be aware of your thinking processes, and you will learn to guard thoughts that are not for your highest good or humanity's.

Esteem, regard, consider, and think about yourselves as individuals. In this world, sometimes it is difficult to esteem ourselves as unique and special. We are part of the whole, we have come from God, and we shall return to God. Remember that we are all unique and special children.

My Son's life was not in vain. Yes, He was misunderstood at times and, yes, He was rebuked. But He walked the path of our Lord, and I encourage you to walk Christ's path.

Think on what is pure and holy and good. I ask you to make a list of seven spiritual values and to think about one each day. Try to progress closer to the mark, closer to that particular spiritual value.

Remember, read the Bible. Read the parables, the Beatitudes. Read what my Son did in His walk.

Take spiritual values and hold them with love like you would a baby, like you would a new seed that is about to be planted for humanity. Count your blessings. Remember to praise God and be in thankfulness. Praise the Lord, for He is mighty and He loves you very much.

There are many earth changes coming. There will be mighty quakes. There will be trembling of the earth. There will be famine as you have never seen. But I tell you to stand firm with your spiritual values. Unite together. Unite together and regard what is good. Regard what your Heavenly Father wants you to do. Remember, He does love you unconditionally.

In the next ten-year period there will be a war; but I tell you do not be confused about it, for the evil one is about and is right now loose on the earth plane. There are two paths that lie ahead. One is the path of the evil one, which is selfish, self-indulged, confused, fearful, and angry. I want you to look to the other path. I want you to look to the path that will save your souls.

Look to the Savior to help you do that. The good path, of course, produces good fruits, produces good works. The good path promotes love, joy, peace, and productivity in all the beautiful ways.

In your heart, know that choices must be made as you approach the new millennium. You must decide which path to take. Make it a conscious decision, please, for it is not too late to choose God's path, Christ's path.

I come to you in tenderness. I come to you as your Mother. I come to you full of grace. I have heard many prayers, and I have taken many to the Creator, and to my Son. Now I ask of you again to stay in your prayer time, to follow us on the path to glory to the throne of grace.

Be gentle with yourselves. Every thought, every decision, is your own. Your Lord has given you free choice and free will to decide which path to take. I encourage you to do what the Lord wishes of you. You are loved, you are regarded, and you are considered as His own.

Forget not the Almighty and His good works towards you. I tell you to remain in a position of receiving God's knowledge for your life, receiving what God's mission is for you, to receive His Holy Call. For eternal life awaits you, as we are united in one common bond — that of love. Remember, perfect love casts out fear and doubt and anger, and all that is unlike God.

I encourage you, then, to regard spiritual values, to think about them, to consider them daily. I also encourage you to pray daily. Say the rosary. Walk in nature. Commune with the Lord. Meditate upon what is God's way, what is Christ's way.

I acknowledge you as my own. I love you all. God's grace be upon you. May His peace come into your hearts. May you choose the right path. May you choose His path. God's blessings be upon you.

Meditation

You are all my babes, my children. I hold you suspended in my arms of love. You are surrounded with divine, pure love from me and my Son, the Christ. As I held Him in my arms and gazed into His eyes, I knew the world would be a better place. Joy has come to the world — we have a Redeemer.

Remember the trust and the innocence of children. Please pray for the children — they are our future and hope. Let not your hearts be troubled, neither let them be afraid. I protect my children through the power of the Holy Spirit. Remember, you have all been children and most of you need great healing. Call upon the Lord for your healing. Let our Father hold you in His mighty arms of love and gently rock you. Do not be afraid. Remember to remain "childlike in spirit." Be tender with yourselves. There is great hope now on this earth plane; there is a new dawning of peace. Please do not harden your hearts. Remember the birth of my precious Son.

Take a moment to center. Relax your shoulders. Close your eyes and take in several deep breaths. Relax your mind. Now, see a baby, vulnerable and precious. This is your "inner child." Reach out and embrace this precious one. Hold him or her lovingly in your arms and gaze into the eyes. What do you see? How do you feel holding the baby? What a miracle of life you are looking at, a miracle from God! Accept and love yourselves now. Forgive yourselves and release the past. Be in the moment. Truly love the baby you are holding and with this be healed.

The Nativity Prayer

O Most Holy Father who created Heaven and Earth,

thank you for Your Son, Jesus Christ.

We honor the Blessed Virgin Mary for Her obedience to You.

We honor Your Son, the Christ, who bore our sins

so that we might be saved.

Thank you for bringing joy, salvation, and hope

to our struggling world.

Bless all the babies and children this day.

Keep them safe Lord, in your Mighty Arms.

Hold them suspended in perfect love.

Keep them from harm and temptation.

They are our future.

Let all your children feel special and loved.

We were all carved and formed from Your Hands.

We are Your "handiwork."

Let us have childlike hearts to see the world in purity and wonder.

Let us all love again, unconditionally, as young children.

Let us honor our earthly fathers and mothers all the days of our lives.

Let us forgive family members who have hurt us,

and let us walk a Christ-like path.

We ask this in faith and love.

Amen.

Archangel Raphael on "The Nativity"

"The Nativity" symbolizes joy to the world, a Savior is born. You are redeemed. You are loved. You are immortal. Your sins have been cleansed and forgiven. Praise the Lord. This was the most divinely ordained event in the history of mankind. For as you know there have been many apostles, prophets, and ascended masters; but there is only one Jesus, the Christ — Jesus of Nazareth.

Notice the tender look on Mary's face as She holds Her newborn. There should be no greater joy to a mother than to have her own child, and we know that this brought great joy to Mary. I tell you that there is no love like a mother's love for her child. This is truly a great compassionate type of love.

Although I am not formally mentioned in the New Testament, I was with the Christ when He was performing His healing work. He walked among you in compassion, humility, and obedience. He walked among you in faith. He did great works with healing. He healed the blind, the mute. He cast out demons. Therefore, this painting is very important to me as Raphael, but also it is important to the world. Gaze upon it with joy in your hearts. If you are doing healing work — physicians, nurses, anyone in the healing profession — call upon my name, archangel Raphael.

I am also the joy bringer. Therefore, yes, I was hovering around the stable when our Christ was born, overseeing the birthing angels. It was a rather easy and effortless birth. As Mary gazes on Her newborn infant, She knows that Christ will bring hope to the world and that you will be saved — eternally loved again in God's Kingdom.

It was a cold and starry night the eve of our Christ's birth. The star in the upper right, the eight pointed star, represents a sign for those on the earth plane; you will rise also to the stars and to the heavens, undaunted and eternally protected and loved in God's Kingdom. For this is the star of hope. It is the star of light. I am the angel of light on the earth plane.

Of the series of twelve paintings, this is one of the greatest, for it denotes happiness and joy that wells up from our hearts. There is a sweeping circular motion that starts behind Mary's head, flowing around Her, and underneath the Christ child, before rising up again. It is a beautifully sweeping circle. It represents eternal love. There is no beginning and no ending to God's love for us, for He loves us totally, unconditionally. The circle is a power symbol. Upon the birth of our Savior a bright beam of light shone down into Mary. The *star of the east*, the Star of Bethlehem, shone brighter than any star that has ever been known, for again it was a starry night on the eve of our Christ's birth. It was very peaceful, although the town was very crowded, and many were talking into the wee hours of the morning. You could hear their voices in the distance. Mary and Joseph were alone with some animals in the stable.

Toward the new millennium many miracles will abound, as there is a healing wave now throughout the globe. Many are coming into the light. Many hearts have been filled with joy. Look for your miracle and you shall receive it! Be healed in the name of our Christ, the star of light and joy for us all.

I especially care for children. They see the world through the eyes of wonder. They love unconditionally. They do not judge. They are creative and imaginative. Yes, there is a healing property about children. Children can heal us through their love. We can also heal ourselves through our "inner child," which gives back to us unconditional love. Christ did say *unless we become as children we cannot enter the Kingdom!* This means loving unconditionally, bringing joy to ourselves and to others. Joy to the world! Protect your inner child, love it, and let it out to play. Forgiveness for anything that you have ever done to harm yourself, or another, will be released through healing your inner child.

Be joyful as a child at play. Look to the stars for your own creative pursuits. Know that you are here on a mission, that you're all here to do something good with your lives. You all have talents, large or small. You need to share those talents. Open your hearts to bring joy to the world, to heal yourself, and to heal others. There will be a new birthing from the year 2000 on. Yes, there will be earth changes, many of them. But I tell you that these paintings are signs that there is a greater life ahead — a divinely ordained life for each and every soul.

Stretch out your hands and bring joy to the world. Share what God has given you as Christ shared for us — His blood and everything He had and everything He was — in honor of Our Heavenly Father.

Three is the number of protection and of the Holy Trinity. Painting number three, "The Nativity," symbolizes the birth of Christ. This was the manifestation of the power of the Father, the Son, and the Holy Spirit unto the earth plane — the power of the three.

The Baptism

Mary's Message

You are born to be reborn; to be

one with spirit, our Creator. By God's

grace you are purified, sanctified, and

forgiven. Baptize and anoint yourselves

with love. There is only love. You

are perfected in God.

Description of Painting

Christ was baptized to cleanse us of our sins. In the fourth painting, water designates our fluid, soul-conscious mind, and the scallop shell means rebirth into the next dimension — Heaven. We are now in a time of rebirthing our planet into light. The shell is a sacred emblem that means cleansing, purification, and the perfection of God's creation.

The small beam of light above Mary's head means alignment with our Higher Creative Source — the godhead. "The Baptism" painting also represents flow and release, unity, and integration with the universe and God. The soft blue-green tones inspire your healing and renewal.

Background

Luke 3:21-22

Now when all the people were baptized, and when Jesus also had been baptized and was praying, Heaven was opened, and the Holy Spirit descended upon Him in bodily form, as a dove, and a voice came from Heaven: "Thou art my beloved Son; with thee I am well pleased."

Mary's Lesson

Painting number four, "The Baptism," symbolizes *purification* and *renewal — the renewal of right spirit within us*. Help us each day, Father, to start again.

I encourage all of you to release what is unlike God. You learn from your past. You cannot forget your past; but remember with each new dawning, with each new day, comes a new opportunity to fill your hearts with joy, a new opportunity for hope, for starting over. God gives you each new day to be able to clear out what is unlike Him, to be able to move closer to His divinity.

I encourage you, then, to put purity in your heart. The pure in heart do not judge. The pure in heart accept God's call. The pure in heart remain childlike, for as you know, unless you become as children, you cannot enter the Kingdom. The pure in heart love unconditionally.

I ask you to baptize yourself in God's holy water. I encourage you to anoint yourself with God's good works. Be disciples of our Creator, our Lord. Follow my Son, Jesus, in your mission in life.

Faith is the ability to overcome obstacles. Let faith be renewed daily in your heart. Let there be a renewal and a joy such as you have never felt before.

The waters of life may rock you at times. You may feel that there are many rocks and obstacles in the water, but I tell you that my Son will chart your course. He will help to guide you through the rocky waters. Have faith to know that you will arrive safely in God's domain.

Heal yourselves! Think of the healing flow of love. We are capable, through the power of God, to heal all that has happened, and to rejoice in the new day, in the new dawning.

I give you a vessel of holy water. I anoint you as my blessed children. I put a drop into your heart to make it pure and clean. I put a drop at your forehead for pure and clean thoughts. I put a drop of holy water at your throat so that you speak good words. I put holy water at each palm, in each hand, for you to produce what your Creator inspires you to produce. I put holy water at your feet, so that as you trod and walk through this journey, this lifetime, this path, you walk in faith and not by sight; you walk forward towards the glory of God.

Be anointed; be purified; be cleansed. Release what is not for your highest good. You will know what to release, because anything that is not of God and not for your highest good will not be accepted unto yourself.

Pray for discernment. Pray to be released from old habits that may pull you down, old ways that you have outgrown. You are ever-evolving and moving towards the sun, towards the light, towards the purification and cleansing that you so desire.

Start each day with a prayer in your heart for renewal. Each new dawning, each waking moment, provides you with opportunities for growth.

With you we are well pleased. Many, many have heard the call and have acknowledged Christ into their hearts. Many have stood strong in their convictions for the Lord. Many have been unswerving in their faith and devotion.

Think of ways in which you can purify your life — in your eating habits, in your patterns, in your thought processes. I tell you that self-discipline is a value.

So I encourage you to purify, to cleanse what is not of God. Through self-discipline, through awareness, move forward. Be kind and gentle with yourselves.

Bathing is important insofar as it releases toxins from the body and also releases unclean thoughts around us. When you bathe, think of the anointing waters, the blessed waters, coming down upon you — blessings from Heaven, purification descending upon you — clearing out what is unlike God and renewing and regenerating what is of God.

Take time for yourselves. Take time for reflection. Take time for prayer. Take time for relaxation. Even my Son spent time away — 40 days and 40 nights in the wilderness — and He was alone in the garden at the end. He knew He needed time to commune with God, His Father. I encourage you to take time for yourselves to commune with God, your Father. Go to your private garden. Pray. Meditate. Think on these things.

As a whole, all are one, but each individual makes up a part of the whole. Each thought, word, and deed, of course, is recorded. It is etched in your soul memory and also, of course, in God's.

Praise the Lord for a second chance, for a new day dawning. Think about your life and where you have been. Think about where you want to go. Look to Christ as your Lord, as your Savior. Accept Him, accept His path.

The pure in heart shall see God. Remain childlike and humble. Know that you are never alone, that in your daily walk and your times of renewal and cleansing, that God's love goes with you. His blessings are upon you.

Man has always battled at times for supremacy, but you need to accept each other. Know that all are equal in God's eyes; that all are created — and life is breathed into all of you — so that you can glorify our Father in Heaven.

Start each day anew. Upon arising, drink a glass of distilled water. Stand near a window. Look at the open sky. Take a walk in nature. Think of spring. Think of God's awakening. Put spring into your heart. Try to suppress the anxieties of the day. I encourage you to learn to relax, for stress and overworking produce anxiety, and anxiety cuts off the flow of love back to yourselves.

I love you my blessed children. I give you my motherly, unconditional love. Sleep in peace and awaken at each new day with enthusiasm for a new beginning and with praise in your heart for the Lord.

Meditation

From the cosmos of the Creator, all life was created. From the depths of the cosmic waters, life was breathed into man. Return again to the waters for purification, renewal, and baptism. You will be washed clean in the "Blood of the Lamb" — my Son's blood.

Ponder all forms of life in a new way — every snowflake, every dew drop, every grain of sand. All is from our Heavenly Father. You are starting to shift your consciousness into a new dimension in preparation for your ascension and my Son's return. Love is the key for releasing all that binds us in our fears. Be purified in the "clean waters" of life. Baptize yourselves daily through thoughts of love, patience, and purity. Thoughts are very powerful, my children — as is prayer. Purify your thoughts, stay in your prayer and meditation time. You have come from the Divine and you will rest in the gentle waters of the Divine.

Balance yourself and sit comfortably. Roll your shoulders backwards a few times. Take several deep breaths and close your eyes. Think of a scallop shell — its perfection and symmetry. See its white smooth surface and its scalloped edge. Use the shell for your *point of contact* and meditate on cleansing — cleansing your body of disease; cleansing your emotions of anger, fear, stress, and worry; cleansing your spirit from anything that is unlike God. Release now that which is unlike God. Take a few moments to let go. Take a few more deep breaths. Hold the scallop shell at your forehead and think of love as perfection. Everything is working now at its own time, in its own way for God's glory. Now see yourself surrounded by a blue-green light. This is a healing and tranquil light. This light will cleanse and purify you. Now, be in God's perfect peace.

The Baptism Prayer

Dear Lord, Maker of Heaven and earth,

we come to You this day in humility.

We pray for cleansing in a greater way!

Cleanse us from past hurts and abuses.

Cleanse us from fear, anger, and anything that is unlike You, Father.

Let us know we can be forgiven, as we forgive others;

that we can be healed as we pray and give healing love to others,

and that we can be balanced

and made whole in all areas of our lives.

Let us be "baptized in Your word," knowing Your will for our lives.

Help us to lead others to You and Your Son, Jesus.

Jesus was baptized and the power of Your Holy Spirit fell upon Him.

Let the power of Your spirit fall upon us in our daily walk.

Give us hope for our ongoing journey in life.

We love You, O Most Gracious Father.

We ask these things in Your Name

and in the name of Your Son, the Blessed Jesus.

Amen.

Archangel Michael on "The Baptism"

The first painting I oversee is painting number four. It is called "The Baptism." This painting is very cosmic. There is a lot of water in the painting, and as you look at it, it looks interdimensional. The scallop shell represents purity of purpose. It is divinely created, a perfected object in nature, for all are divinely created from God. Below the scallop shell is a colored shape very similar to the sign of infinity, for this is a painting of infinity. You will all be cleansed from unrighteousness now in this time, in this day, in this age.

I am the mighty angel of purification. I help those that pray, to come to the light. I help hearts to be cleansed and purified. I help thoughts to be cleansed and purified, for this is my divine mission, and this is what the Creator created me to do. This painting symbolizes renewal and purification. It is infinite. It will live forever in hearts that are cleansed.

There will be a reawakening in Germany of those that are coming to the light, those that are being cleansed and purified. During the Holocaust, I, archangel Michael, helped many souls to the light. As you know, there was great wailing and anguish. It was one of the greatest travesties in history. There is going to be a gentle new cleansing in the country of Germany. This, humanity will understand later.

The all seeing, the all wise, the all powerful, the omnipotent, loving Creator has ordained these paintings. When you gaze on "The Baptism," you will enter a new cosmic dimension of soul-mind communication with the Creator. There will be a feeling of a new awakening. There will be a total release of pain, emotional torment, anguish, stress, and anxiety.

"The Baptism," again, does not necessarily represent our
Lady's face. Five of the twelve paintings portray female saints.
This face is one of the most etheric and ethereal, for it looks
through the dimensions. The eyes are filled with love.

Notice in the painting, there are no hard edges. All the
strokes flow and circulate. They are very gentle, flowing lines.
There is also a gentleness about this painting, an essence reminding
one of water — the soul-mind consciousness.

When you walk along the edge of the ocean you see many
shells, for all are God's creation. One of the most beautiful, most
perfected shells is the scallop shell. Every line is perfect in its
design. It has a gentle curve at the top that tapers down to one
point. It has many ridges, and yet all are contained in one beautiful
object. It represents unity, cleansing, purification. It comes from
the water. Our Divine Mother chose this as the meditation symbol
for this particular painting.

I encourage those who find "The Baptism" their favorite painting,
to soak in water. You might want to take cleansing baths — baths
of purification. Rosemary might be sprinkled into the bath water.
Chamomile, rose oil, or lavender would also be good. This will
cleanse your aura or the energy field around your physical body.
The physical body is your solid body, flesh and blood. The aura is
a field of energy that protects you.

At times, if you are weak in your emotional link, you will
imbibe other people's energy. Energy means thoughts. Energy
means emotions. This can be good if the other individual is
positive, filled with joy and love and happiness; but it can also
be negative when the other individual's energy field is filled with
fear, anger, and anxiety. Therefore, it is very important on a weekly
basis to make the time — to discipline yourself to take the time —

to sit in a soaking bath. It is true, Epsom salts do tend to relax the muscles, but too many Epsom salt baths pull water from the human body. Therefore, if you choose to take Epsom salt baths during the week, you need to drink more water, preferably distilled water — at least ten to fifteen glasses a day — to replace the water that has been taken from the body.

Here is my advice for soaking baths as given to me by the Creator and our Lady. Make sure you are alone, in privacy. You might want to burn a rose pink candle or a white candle. Rose pink is the color of healing love, our Lady's color. White is the color of cleansing and purification. Again, sprinkle soothing herbs into the bath water. Soak for approximately one hour, clearing the mind of any worry, confusion, doubt, or fear. This would be a good time to think of the water as being energizing and purifying, as it also helps to cleanse the aura around the human body.

Water has always had a cleansing and a healing property. If you could take time to go to the ocean, a lake, or even a stream or a river, it would be conducive for your healing and cleansing. As I protect the globe, I also oversee the grottoes, the energy of lakes, oceans, streams, and rivers. You will find me there. Our Lady will also be there. She has many times appeared where there was water. Many shrine sites, such as Lourdes, which have been dedicated to our Lady, have water. Even Michele's "Madonna of the Towel" (see picture in "Michele's Story") manifested beside the tub. The tub represents the baptismal font — a place for healing and the cleansing power of the Holy Spirit.

"The Baptism" painting signifies a time when Christ was baptized. He was baptized to further cleanse us from our sins. He was baptized in the power of the Holy Spirit which fell upon Him like a dove from Heaven. He was baptized to give hope to humanity. All can receive graces and blessings through the power of the cleansing waters of the Holy Spirit, for water represents the power of the Holy Spirit.

You might want to bring water into your home, perhaps in the form of a small tabletop fountain, or even a lovely bowl filled with distilled water. You might want to float flowers in a bowl, along with burning white candles which represent cleansing and purity. These are good ways to bring angelic energy into the home.

The colors in this painting are very important. Remember, blue is a healing color and so is green. There will be many healings from the viewing of painting number four, "The Baptism." It will vibrate with the energy of those that are ill, especially those with heart problems, for green vibrates with the chest region. Blue-green or aqua vibrates with the lower throat region. Wearing these colors is also helpful, for you imbibe the colors that you wear into your aura.

When you enter the body at birth, your soul comes in through the top of the head with pure white, blinding light. Purple is the highest spiritual color. It vibrates with the forehead region which is synonymous with the seat of intuition. Royal blue or indigo blue vibrates with the lower face region. Aqua or blue-green is with the throat region. Emerald green vibrates with the chest region or heart region. Yellow is the abdomen area, the solar plexus. Orange resonates with the reproductive area. Red represents the limbs. Your legs ground you or bind you to the earth through gravity.

When you do healing work, you need to wear shades of blue-green. When you ask for healing you also need to wear blue-green. These colors are healing, as this painting is healing.

My essence, the mighty archangel Michael, will come through the painting of "The Baptism." I protect this beautiful painting for it is one of my favorites. This painting will cleanse and clear out emotional distress. The longer you gaze upon this painting, the more emotions will be released. Remember to look at it with an open mind. Remember the flow of the cosmic waters.

So again I say to humanity, this painting is very cosmic and very healing. Use the meditation wisely. Think of the scallop shell as a *point of contact*. Think of your soul as being infinite. You are created to glorify our Creator, to glorify our Heavenly Father, our God.

Painting number four, "The Baptism," represents balance. Four is an even, symmetrical number. Two plus two equals four. "The Baptism" symbolizes the need for purification. Cleanse out the old that you no longer need. It means balancing your life in all areas.

Balance the spiritual muscles. This has to do again with prayer and meditation time. Know that you are on an eternal journey and that the journey is never-ending — for learning, growing, and becoming more Christ-like — becoming like our Savior.

All souls need to purify areas of their lives and release what is not for their highest good, and release that which inhibits the progress of their spiritual journey.

Drink distilled water. Take walks in nature. Read good literature. Do good deeds. Stay in your prayer and meditation time. Guard, cleanse, and purify the physical and emotional planes.

There are many ways to purify the emotional plane of existence. First of all, bring back to yourself the unconditional love that you give others. Be kind and gentle with yourself. Pace yourself. Take time for rest and relaxation. That is balance.

The Communion

Mary's Message

The sharing and unification of
spirit and souls is what God requests
of you. You are to unite as one in love and
peace. You are to commune with each other; to
be one in all and all in one. My Son shared
His Body and Blood for you all. Have
Communion and remember the
purpose of the Last Supper.

Description of Painting

"The Communion" represents the Last Supper of Christ with His disciples before His Crucifixion. "The chalice (sometimes called the Holy Grail) and Host are symbols that remind us of the Blessed Sacrament. The chalice or cup signifies the precious Blood of Christ"[4] and symbolizes abundance; the endless flow of receiving God's grace. It denotes a *spiritual vessel* that holds the life force and represents quest and discovery of self. "The Host (or circle above it) represents the Sacred Body."[5]

The circles, swirls, and dove overhead mean eternal alignment and peace; the violet light above Mary's head is a healing light that permeates our being.

Background
Matthew 26:26-29

Now as they were eating, Jesus took bread, blessed, and broke it, and gave it to the disciples and said, "Take, eat; this is my Body." Then He took a cup, and when He had given thanks, he gave it to them, saying, "Drink of it, all of you; for this is my Blood of the covenant, which is poured out for many for the forgiveness of sins. I tell you I shall not drink again of this fruit of the vine until that day when I drink it new with you in my Father's Kingdom!"

Mary's Lesson

Painting number five, "The Communion," means *unity* and *oneness*. My Son, the Christ, communed with His disciples at the end. He shared His thoughts with them. He shared His body, His Blood, symbolically. He shared all that He was. He shared His love from the Creator with them.

I ask you to commune with one another; to share the good word of the Lord; to share your experiences, your joys, your hopes, your trials; to unite together; to unite in love; and, to unite for a common goal.

Your goal is to grow closer towards the Lord. Commune and share the good that has happened in your lives. Humanity needs, now more than ever, to be encouraged, to be uplifted, to be ennobled. Share what has been good and uplifting with your fellow man. Remember, it is sometimes the small and insignificant things that we do that make the greatest difference.

My Son, as He walked His path, was a good teacher. He healed from the power of His Father. He healed through love. He shared His knowledge of our Lord. He knew that He could not touch the whole world physically in His short lifetime, but He knew He had to plant seeds.

His followers have taken those seeds forward and the Lord's word has grown and grown. There are many converts now to the word of our God and to the word of my Son, the Christ.

I tell you, then, to share what is good; share with your fellow man on your daily walk what would give them hope, what would lighten their hearts. There are many ways to share: your time, your talents, your energies. But I tell you, it is the little things — it is the smiles, it is the sharing — that are most important on a daily basis. Be kind to strangers. Put kindness as a spiritual value in your heart. Judge not.

The story of my Son, Jesus, has been shared throughout the world; and as it has been shared, people have experienced new hope. I ask of you to make it a point to share something of yourself and the Lord's good works with someone on a daily basis.

You do not need to go out of your way to serve. You can serve where you are. You can begin where you are. If you are housebound, then smile upon the mailman. If you are in the busy workplace, remember once a day to share a good thought with a fellow worker.

As you share, you unify. You become whole and one in a common thread, which is love. Love is sharing; therefore, I ask you to share God's love with someone each day. On your commute to and fro, do not forget that the Lord is ever present. The power of communion is in oneness — a common thought and a common thread for the good of the whole.

I also encourage you commune with yourselves on a daily basis; go inward; touch that still inner voice; touch that inner knowing that you have of God. Commune with others, but also commune with yourself. Set time aside for meditation. Go to a quiet place. Pray, meditate, ponder. Ponder what is good. Ponder where you need to be as an individual in the whole of creation.

Remember, the Lord's love has no bounds. You need to love yourself and bring back the love that you give to others, by spending time communing with yourself, by being whole and one within your own heart — within yourself. Then you can give more completely and freely to others around you.

I encourage you to pray and commune with God. Ask what His purpose is and His will for your life. Listen. God's answers may at times be direct, but they also come in mysterious ways, sometimes when we least expect them.

Drink water. Fill up your cups. Know that you are here to have life and have it more abundantly. For this is a painting of abundance. As the cup of life fills, it also overflows and that is where sharing comes in; sharing our cups, one with another, our precious thoughts, our good works, our talents. Fill each other's cup as you fill your own.

Water has a very cleansing property. There are radioactive particles in the air in this world, and there are contaminants, so I encourage you to drink more distilled water. It will purify your body. It will open your soul and mind to the higher power, which is our Lord. Many of you house toxins in your body. Drinking water is purifying. It will assist you with opening yourselves to receive not only love, not only grace, but information from God.

Remember that my Son, the Christ, died for you; He shed His Blood for you. Remember the Last Supper, the Eucharist, and what it means. Reach out. Touch someone in your daily walk. Walk the path of my Son.

Blessings on all of you. You are here to have life and have it more abundantly. Remember, God's love knows no bounds. There are limitless possibilities for your own spiritual growth towards our Lord. Have abundance. Appreciate what is yours. Value what God has given you. Give Him praise and give Him glory. And remember, your cup runneth over with love, with abundance. For His love is infinite and boundless and abundant. So peace be with all of you. Peace be in your hearts. God's blessings be upon you.

Meditation

I, Blessed Mother, have come to share and commune with you. Take the cup of abundance — the "Holy Grail." It contains the *life force* — the Blood of my Son, the Christ, shed for your eternal salvation. We need to spread the word to humanity that there is hope, that we can change the course of this world through our thoughts, deeds, and prayer time. Commune with me, my Son, and our Holy Father.

Share the gospel, the good news of my Son's return to this earth. He is coming in holy glory to rapture His beloved ones into the Kingdom. Share yourselves with each other in love. Remember the time is at hand to take the cup, to accept my Son, Jesus, into your hearts. Please accept Him now. The time for the ascension of humanity is at hand.

Sit straight and relaxed in your chair. Uncross your legs. By deep breathing, you release the stress of the day. Close your eyes and center yourself. See in front of you a beautiful shining cup or chalice. It contains all your dreams and heart's desires. What does it look like? See it in your mind's eye, in every detail. I, Blessed Mother, personally hand you your cup. What does it feel like in your hand? Now, drink from it and commune with us. You are now *sharing* the glory, honor, and peace of God. Take a few moments to relish in this communion. I now give you bread, the Host, which represents my Son's Body. Put it symbolically on your tongue. Christ is now within you — you are one with us. May God's grace be upon you.

The Communion Prayer

Dear Lord,

We accept the Holy Communion Cup with respect and honor.

Thank you for letting Your Son, Jesus,

share His Body and Blood with us.

Thank you for sending us a Savior, for loving us that much.

If we feel unworthy or dejected, lift us up Father,

to where we should be.

Let us remember our Most Gracious Virgin Mary —

our Mother who accepted first Your "Holy Call."

Then let us remember Jesus,

who bore great pain for our cleansing.

Let us keep the concept of "Holy Communion"

— the Eucharist — in our hearts and soul,

the holy Body and Blood of Christ, our Savior.

Let us also remember You, dear Father,

and Your concern, love, and protection toward us.

Help us to do Your will, in obedience and reverence.

Never has there been such love bestowed upon man,

as when Your Son died for us!

Let us honor and remember all that is true.

We ask this in humility and thankfulness.

Amen.

Archangel Raphael on "The Communion"

This is archangel Raphael. I was assigned to oversee, protect, vibrate with, and lend my healing energy to painting number five, "The Communion."

I am the angel of prayer. I work with our Lady, the Blessed Mother, when prayers are said. She intercedes every prayer and takes them to Her Son, the Christ, and to our Heavenly Father. No prayer goes unheard or unanswered. Millions of prayers are said at one time and are all received through Blessed Mother. She blesses each and every prayer through Her divine, feminine, healing essence. As each prayer is blessed, it becomes very empowering, and it is greatly noticed then by Her Son, the Christ, and greatly heard by God, the Father.

Prayer is very powerful, as thought forms are powerful. Prayer is different from meditation. Meditation is the "stilling of the mind." Prayer is "reaching out with our hearts through love to our Creator." It is extending thoughts out toward the Creator, in praise and thanksgiving. Prayer is also used to ask the Creator for help in the troublesome areas of your lives.

A very powerful prayer is the "I am" prayer. God is the great I am, that I am, that I am. Therefore, realize that in prayer time if human beings would say the "I am," it would empower them with the Christ Consciousness. It would remind them of God's eternal love. It is a simple prayer, yet powerful, and it goes as such:

I am in the light of God. I am God's creation. I am in unconditional love. I am in peace. I am in joy. I am in wholeness.

But any prayer — large or small, simple or complex — is heard. In fact, God knows your thoughts before you think them for He created you!

Prayers are interesting. As I have traveled the earth, I have noticed that each individual prays in a different manner. Children give beautiful prayers. They are simple, and they are real. Prayers should not in any way be manipulative, for God sees the heart of the one praying. For example, some people feel that they need to barter with God. You do not have to give up anything to receive Gods grace, love, attention, or protection.

Painting number five, "The Communion," symbolizes oneness with God in prayer time. It represents sharing with God, all in one and one with all.

To pray, you can kneel beside your bed. Walking in nature is a wonderful way to pray. Praying at the same time each day, structures the mind. As we have observed from the angelic kingdom, human beings tend to be habitual. You tend to find comfort in the safety of habit. Therefore, if you discipline yourself to say your prayers in the morning, (even if it is driving to work in the morning), or at dusk when you walk in nature, it is fine.

It is important to commune with God daily, and it is important to commune with others daily — to share your time, your talents, and your energy with others. Individuals might say "I have no talent. I have no gifts." Spiritual gifts, though, come in many forms. Remember, it's the simplest of gifts that are the most dynamic — a smile, a hug, a loving thought, a card in the mail, a remembrance. These are gifts that well up in the heart and are shared. Remember to share what you have with others. This does not mean material possessions or money; it just means to share love.

Communion is a wonderful thing. At the Last Supper, Christ communed with His disciples. He shared His love for His disciples and for all mankind, as He shared His Body and His Blood. As Christ sat with His twelve disciples, and He broke bread, He said, "Take, eat, this is my Body, this is given for you. Do this in remembrance of me." Then Christ took a cup filled with wine. He offered it to His disciples. "Take, drink, this is my Blood that is shed for you."

Remember our Savior, remember that He gave up His life so that you might have life and have it more abundantly. Your sins, although they be as scarlet, are washed as white as snow in the Blood of the Lamb. Every sin is recorded in the book of life. Remember, angels and archangels do not sin. We have never been human. We do not judge. I, Raphael, am not judging when I say this. I am merely observing that you are in the human condition to experience sin, to become aware of sin, and to be cleansed from all unrighteousness.

This painting, "The Communion," is a very peaceful painting. For Christ had peace to know that although He would suffer great agony and pain on the cross, He would rise victorious. Therefore, in this painting, our Lady is looking into the cup or chalice with a very peaceful expression on Her face. She knew in Her heart that Her Son would overcome death, and rise into a realm of immortality, eternal life.

The chalice is shining. It symbolically contains Christ's Blood, the life force. Above the cup is the Host, which represents Christ's Body. On the left side of the Host, there is a white crescent. The crescent moon is one of Mary's symbols. It personifies the love, nurturing, creative, and intuitive facets of the feminine, divine spirit. There is also a crescent moon above our Blessed Mother's head.

Actually of the twelve paintings, five of them contain crescent moons. Again, this is symbolic of feminine, divine healing. White is the highest spiritual color, meaning it vibrates with the upper dimensions. There also is a circular white symbol on the left side of the painting. This represents eternal love, no beginning and no ending, for God's love is eternal.

The white form in the middle of the painting looks like a dove; but in fact it is two doves, one facing slightly to the left, and one facing toward the right. Depending on how you view the painting, you will see both doves contained within. They represent the power of the Holy Spirit.

The two crescent moons and the two doves represent balance. If you look at the stem of the chalice, you will also see two rubies. They denote not only two drops of Christ's Blood that have been shed, but also represent the Body of Christ — perfect harmony and balance for humanity. They represent unity and equality among all races, peoples, nations, cultures, and religions. You are all God's children, and you are all equal in God's sight. You are all equal in our Savior's sight and also in Mary's.

These symbols are a reminder to balance your physical selves with good nutrition. Be aware of those things that are for your highest good to consume. Drink distilled water which cleanses the body of all toxins and impurities. Get physical exercise, walk in nature, and breathe deeply. Spend time in meditation and prayer. Learn to bring the unconditional love that you give to others back to yourselves. Learn to be kind and gentle with yourselves. You have come from God, and you need to take time to commune with yourselves along with communing with others.

You can commune with yourselves in many different ways — in the quiet, in the stillness, behind closed doors. Those are good times to say prayers, for our Heavenly Father who made you in secret sees you in secret and hears your prayers in secret.

If you can physically get to a church, then I encourage you to take Holy Communion. Partake in the Eucharist, take the bread of life which is Christ's Body into yourselves. Take the wine which is Christ's Blood into your body. If you are ill and cannot make it to a holy place such as a church, then take Communion in your home. It's the love, that you show through obedience to our Creator by remembering Communion, that is so important.

This is a very hopeful painting, and even though our Lady did not share with the disciples in the Last Supper, She understood the full impact of Her Son's dying. Notice that the color purple is greatly used in this painting. It is an empowering color; therefore, you are empowered by the blood shed and the body bruised of our Christ, empowered because He has taken on your sins.

I, Raphael, am drawn to this painting because it reminds me of unity of thought, unity of world peace, all people joining hands around the globe, speaking the same language symbolically. The universal language of humanity and oneness is love. It is as simple as that.

So, this is Raphael, archangel of healing and prayer, encouraging humanity to stay in prayer time, to think of the Holy Communion as Christ's word that you are cleansed of your sins. Remain faithful to our Heavenly Father. Remember that you are loved eternally and unconditionally, now and evermore.

Painting number five, "The Communion," represents divinity, unity, and oneness with God. It is the painting of the communion — of coming together and giving and sharing.

Five is the number of sharing and divinity. For when you are in God's grace (which you always are), and when you are aware of God's grace, you are aware of your own divinity. All come from God, God is in you, you are in God, and unto God you shall return.

Five is a powerful number for it represents your soul-mind consciousness in the divinity of God. Therefore, "The Communion" painting was placed in the fifth position because it represents your unification with the Divine, your oneness with the Divine. It calls for you to know and be aware of your own divinity as a united race, as a united culture, as one globe, and as one world.

The Crucifixion

Mary's Message

My Son, the Christ, shed His
blood so that we might live eternally
forgiven in the Kingdom of God. Through His
and my tears of agony, you are cleansed, purified,
and heirs to the throne of grace. To give one's
life, in death for all — there is no
greater love than this.

Description of Painting

Christ dies on the cross after several hours of agony, and Mary weeps sorrowful tears for Her Son. In the sixth painting, the dark purple shade in the background represents the "Passion of Christ" and was painted to make an emotional impact on the viewer.

The faint illuminated cross in the sky symbolizes the divine power of God, "personifies Christ, or faith in Christ. By honoring the sacred cross, we thereby honor Jesus and profess our faith in Him crucified."[6] The three red roses represent the Holy Trinity and Christ's blood shed for our salvation.

Background

Luke 23:33, 44-46

When they came to the place which is called "The Skull," there they crucified Him, and the criminals, one on the right and one on the left. And Jesus said, "Father, forgive them; for they know not what they do."

It was now about the sixth hour, and there was a darkness over the whole land until the ninth hour, while the sun's light failed; and the curtain of the temple was torn in two. Then Jesus, crying with a loud voice said, "Father, into thy hands I commit my spirit!" With these words, He breathed His last.

Mary's Lesson

The painting, "The Crucifixion," means *forgiveness of injuries*. My Son, the Christ, died for all. He gave His life; He gave His blood; He gave His body. Remember, then, the power of the cross.

All, in a lifetime, have crosses to bear. All have pain — physical and emotional. All have suffering at times. But remember that my Son's blood was not shed in vain; that there is power behind the cross.

The cross represents, of course, the agony of my Son; but the cross also foretells what is to come: the resurrection. It symbolizes the ability to overcome obstacles; to forgive injuries; to pardon others.

My Son, the Christ, had great humility. He carried that humility with Him to the very end, and into Heaven. I wept sorrowful tears at the foot of the cross. But I tell you that I weep no more for my Son, for He is with me. He is by my side. We are eternally in God's grace in the realms of light in the heavenly regions.

My children, my precious ones, do not lose hope. When your days are dark, when your mood is down, when you feel abandoned or lonely or rebuked, remember the cross. I inspire you to buy a gold cross and to wear a gold cross. A cross will empower you; it will protect you.

My Son died after many hours of agony. The sky darkened. The winds blew. I watched as every drop of blood drained from his precious body. It was a moment of tremendous anguish and heaviness for me to watch my beloved Son be in pain.

But I tell you, He rose above it, looking to the left and to the right, forgiving those on each side; crying to His Father in Heaven to do the will of His Father and not His own will. The crucifixion, for all — the cross in your own heart, your own crosses to bear — represents an element of patience, nonjudgmental attitude, and forgiveness.

When you look at this painting, "The Crucifixion," you feel the heaviness that was in my heart. The red roses contained in the painting are for the Blessed Trinity, and red is symbolic of my Son's blood. I encourage you, then, to forgive — forgive yourself as you forgive others. Say the Lord's Prayer daily. Remember to forgive.

We are all individuals on the earth plane. We all have problems. We all have weaknesses. Tolerance is the key. Forgiveness of injuries means tolerance — tolerance to live among this world; tolerance not to point a finger at thy neighbor or judge thy friend for what he has done or has not done; tolerance to know that individuals created by God are unique, and each one is different. Each one thinks in a different way, has a different personality, and has a different essence. Let us then be tolerant one to another. Let us abide always in God's vast love.

Patience is synonymous with tolerance. Patience is waiting. Patience is having faith. Patience is a virtue. And I have to say that it took my Son, Jesus, a great deal of patience over His ministry to deal with the intolerant, and to deal with those that judged Him and accused Him. So great was His love for all of us, so tender was His compassion, that He was able — as the Chosen One — to move forward. He was able to pick up His cross, carry it, and bear it — as we all do here on the earth plane — with a sense of hope, knowing that He was doing God's divine will, not only for His life, but for all of humanity.

Remember to open your heart to all of humanity. I encourage you to pray for world peace. Please, pray for the children. The children are our future and our hope. To them, you give your future. Pray daily for those minds, hearts, and souls to come to my Son, the Christ, to be enlightened on their daily walk. Pray for the consciousness — the thought forms of humanity — to rise towards the good, to rise towards our Father in Heaven.

I ask of you, each one of you, to be in a state of God's grace (which you always are), to feel in a state of God's grace as you bear your cross.

My Son died immortal. Many, many were converted immediately after His death. There were great claps and rolls of thunder. And, I tell you, there was a hush over the earth like there has never been before.

I mourned for Him for many, many years after His passing, but I knew in my heart that He was with me, and He was waiting to take me home. Now we are together, as you will be with us.

Remember, the journey may not be easy in this lifetime, but look to the cross! Know that you have a Savior. You have a Redeemer. Reach out your hand and take the hand of my Son,

Christ Jesus. Take His hand. Let Him pull you up and out. Let Him pull you up from ignorance, from intolerance, from a judgmental attitude, from impatience, from boastfulness, from pride. Let Him pull you up and out of your adversities. He is your Redeemer.

I send you "mother love." Mother love is the divine, loving essence of the world. I send it into your hearts to ease your pain. Your pain is temporary, but your Kingdom is neverending. The Kingdom I speak of is the Kingdom with our Lord. As souls, all will unite and join together in perfect harmony — forever in God's Kingdom. Please believe this.

The time now is at hand to become aware of the world, to become aware of all humanity, of all that is. Please, I ask of you, do not harden your hearts. Remember to have faith in your daily walk. Faith does move mountains, but faith also instills within us a sense of peace — for we know that we walk not in our hands by our own might, but with God's might.

Please, I encourage you to forgive yourselves as you forgive others. Self-love is very important — for God is within you. God is love. I say to you, then, forgive yourselves. As I have said many times before — each and every one of you — be kind, be gentle to yourself. Bring back the unconditional love to yourself that you give unto others.

Remember, you are God's chosen ones. He prizes each and every one of you as unique and special. He loves you each individually. Every hair on your head is numbered. God knows about your every thought. He knows what is in your heart. He protects you. He watches your comings and your goings. He watches you arise in the morning. He watches over your daily walk. He gives you peace and sends His angels to you at night.

Peace, my Son gives to you. His peace, I pray, goes into your hearts; not as the world knows peace, but as our Heavenly Father knows peace — true inner peace. True inner peace comes by forgiving others and forgiving yourselves. Forgiveness of injuries is the key — the key to making the transition from the earthly plane to the heavenly plane.

We are in a great movement, a great ascension from the earthly plane into the heavenly plane. The time is now. The time is now to open your hearts to the truth. I bring you, dear children, the truth. The truth is that you are from God, and you shall return to God. The truth is that I am your Heavenly Mother. I love you as much as I loved my own Son, the Christ. There is no love as a mother's love. Remember, this is a healing love.

These paintings are for healing. They are to help with the shift from the earth plane to the heavenly plane. They are paintings of cleansing, purification, and healing. They are also paintings of alignment, to help balance each individual as he or she needs it.

I understand that all have been injured. All have been wounded. All have felt slighted and, at times, abandoned. All have felt alone. But with the power of the cross, you are never alone. The power of the cross is ever constant. It is unfailing. Think of the cross, wear the cross, pray the stations of the cross, pray the rosary. (See appendices.)

I love you with a love that is neverending. I give you God's grace, God's blessings. I tell you that you will have mournful days and you will have joyful days, but remember to be in a state of peace and a state of balance. True balance and peace comes from knowing that you are children of God, that you are protected, that you are overseen, that you are watched and loved.

Try not to measure your standards by those of others. Try to remain firm in your convictions. Please God on a daily basis. Do what is God-like. Please walk the path of my Son, Jesus. Be tender, one to another — compassionate of heart — forgiving — releasing.

In today's world, many are filled with great stresses which they place upon themselves. Financial stress, stress in the workplace, stress at home. Remember to take your stress to God. Put it at His feet. Give it to me. I will help you release your stress.

Think of a beautiful rose. Think of its fragrance of love exuding. Think of the love behind the rose and how it was created for you. Take a minute and reflect about your life, about the things that have happened to you.

If there have been unpleasant things or things that you feel have hurt you, I ask you please to release them — *release them!* Put them in God's hands. For you need to release and let go, and forgive now. Now is the time to do this. I give you the cross. I give you the cross, whether it be wood, gold, silver, jeweled. I give you the cross as a symbol, as our Father's symbol and my Son's symbol of power. True power is love. Remember, there is only love. I give you these lessons for these paintings now, because they are needed now on the earth plane. They are needed to give hope and encouragement to my people and to God's people — to my Son's people.

Come to me all ye that are weary, put your head on my lap. I will soothe your burdens. I will help to ease your stress. I am the great intercessor. I will take your prayers to my Son and to our Heavenly Father. Remember, you do not pray to me. You pray to our Father in Heaven. I am only the intercessor who, by my feminine divine love for you, will take personally each and every prayer said to our Father and my Son.

Remember, your soul is infinite. Your soul is eternal. Your soul is indestructible. Remember, you will be with us in Heaven. Be gentle my children. Remember that we love you very much.

God's blessings be upon you. Take time to respect and revere; remain in reverence to nature, God's creation, to one another and to all that is. This I pray for all of you, my children, that you will come to know my Son as I have, that you will come to know my Lord as I have.

God's peace, grace, and blessings be upon all of you.

Meditation

My Son, the Christ, gave His life for humanity. He was obedient to our Father, as I was obedient in accepting the Call. I wept many times throughout the life of my Son. I wept for joy when He was born. I shed tears of agony and anguish when He was crucified. So great was my love for Him, and so great was His love for you! When the skies become dark around you, my children, when you feel alone with your own cross to bear, remember, we are with you. I give you comfort. We will not leave you alone or desolate. Christ died alone but rose victorious! We are all rising to a Higher Power — our Creator — to be forever in His Kingdom.

Remember the cross — it is a blessed symbol of many things. It personifies Christ's obedience to take on the sins of the world. It represents hope and peace for what is to come.

Relax your mind for a few moments. Remain in the moment. Close your eyes and count in five, slow, deep breaths. Center yourself. Think of a cross in front of you. It is your cross and can be any size and material. What does your cross look like — is it small or large? Is it wood, gold, silver, or some other material? Remember that love stands behind the *power of the cross*. This will always be God's leading symbol for us. Feel the total love and grace emanating from your cross. What does your cross mean for you? The cross also represents a crossroads to healing! Now, release the wounds and hurts from the past — whether they be physical, emotional, mental, or spiritual. You are now a new creature in Christ — glorified. Take a couple more deep breaths. Meditate upon the healing that is now occurring, the healing of your heart. Put your cross into your heart region now. Remember, love heals all.

The Crucifixion Prayer

We pray to the King of Kings and the Lord of Lords!

We pray to our gentle, wise, loving Father.

We all, as humans, must bear some form of pain,

for that is the human condition.

Beyond the pain is glory

because our precious Savior, Jesus, gave His life for us all.

We may weep tears of anguish or joy, during our lifetime, Father,

but let our tears cleanse away

anything that is unlike You, Dear God.

Tears can purify and be healing.

We pray for healing in all areas of our lives.

If we feel tested, betrayed, or alone,

let us know we are in Your protection and mercy.

Your gentle hand guides and directs our footsteps.

We give You the glory, Father, and the praise.

Clouds may be dark at times,

but the power of love shines brighter than the sun

and will break through the darkest clouds.

Darkness will flee. Light and love will prevail.

You are wonderful and wise, O Most Gracious Father.

Thank you for sending Your Son to heal us.

Amen.

Archangel Michael on
"The Crucifixion"

I oversee painting number six, "The Crucifixion." I protect and guard this painting because I am the angel of death. As I said before, I lead souls into eternal light, into the fourth dimension and into their own immortality. I also announced the death of our Lady, our beautiful Mother Mary.

This is a very moving and emotionally impacting painting. It will move hearts, and for some it will bring tears. The deep, heavy, blue tones in the sky represent the darkness that fell on the earth; but there is always hope and light behind the clouds. Our Lady is a strong woman. She knew She was on a mission. She put herself not so much behind the cause, or the Holy Call; but She was obedient unto the call. There is no greater love as a mother for her children — unconditional, true love.

Many will find "The Crucifixion" to be their favorite painting. Many have been hurt throughout childhood, and many can identify with different forms of pain — physical pain, emotional pain, and mental abuses. You are all here to learn. For as I oversee the earth, I see that each individual is on a mission or quest. You have chosen to come to the earth because you have a mission. It took a lot of strength for each and every one of you to come here. One of the most difficult things is to be born. You come from the beautiful heavenly realms into a world with negativity, abuse, physical and emotional pain, and crime. Therefore, you are to be commended because you had the courage to enter your human baby body. I admonish you all, on a daily basis, to release what is not like our Creator, to release what is unlike God. This will assist you on your mission, to keep you in alignment with the Creator's will for you.

"The Crucifixion" stands for everyone to know that Christ followed our Creator's words. He was obedient unto our Creator. He did not turn His back on the world. He fulfilled his mission. Many were converted after our Savior breathed His last breath. Behind the darkness and sadness of this painting there is great hope. For as you know, Christ rose victorious!

The power of the cross is monumental in this painting, for the cross is the symbol that our Lady chose for this meditation. The cross symbolizes all of humanity; you all have your crosses to bear — some are heavy and some are light. You would not be in the earthly dimension if you did not have things to learn, things to do, things to accomplish. God knows all of you individually. He knows your thoughts. He watches your comings and your goings. He is in every heart. God is in you; you are with God constantly.

Remember, our Lady asks you in Her lesson on "The Crucifixion," to wear a cross. A cross will protect all those who wear it, all those who carry it. You might want to put a cross in the glove compartment of your car. You might want to carry a cross in your wallet or in your pocket. It is *best* to wear a cross around your neck. This symbol has deep spiritual meaning; it is not symbolic of a cult or fad.

I speak the truth. My sword cuts through any falsity. My sword represents the truth. See how it shines in the sunlight.

I was there at the time our Savior breathed His last. He said, "Father, into your hands I commend my spirit." Our Savior took my hands as we entered the heavenly realms of the fourth dimension. When our Savior entered the heavenly realms, there was such joy and jubilation. There are angels that sing around the throne of God constantly, singing praises of the Lord. Read the Book of Revelation, and you will understand what I am saying.

In Heaven, we do not have night, nor do we have day. It is just beautiful bright light. Remember that pain is temporary, but our Father's Kingdom is eternal. This is archangel Michael and I bring good tidings to humanity. I also want to say that if you need strength I will be there. If you are fearful — about flying in airplanes, about driving, about your home being broken into, or somebody stealing things from you — call upon me, archangel Michael! I will come in peace, with the true gospel of peace. I will uplift and protect — for that is what I was created to do. I am known above all else, it seems, as the mighty archangel of protection. Some policemen even carry a prayer card of me! I am divinely ordained, and I was created to protect the world as you know it. Remember, however, that no name is above our Creator's name, God Almighty.

The painting, "The Crucifixion," will cause great emotion when you view it. Our Lady is shown with a single tear. This tear is symbolic of all the tears that our Lady has shed. In this particular case Her heart was filled with great pain and agony — watching Her beloved Son, the Christ, die on the cross. The skies darkened. There was a hush over the world as there has never been before.

This painting represents not only death, but immortality. Death is only a passing from one state into another. Death, for human beings, means passing out of the human body. I, archangel Michael, will come to each and every one of you at the time you breathe your last breath. I tell you, people of the world, do not fear death. As you know, the butterfly emerges from the cocoon in all its glory — with beautiful color to fly free! The same is with physical death. It is just another stage of development. You will leave your body, or cocoon, and *fly free in beautiful color!* You will fly free in the heavenly realms. Though you go through the valley of the shadow of death, have no fear. I will be there to assist in your transition from the earthly plane. If you have a friend who is dying, please pray for that friend in the name of our Savior, the Christ. Also, if you ask me, the mighty archangel Michael, I will come to that individual. Call him by name to me, and I will be there to ease his pain at the end time.

Painting number six, "The Crucifixion," represents the power of the Holy Spirit. It represents a divinely blessed event — when Christ gave His life.

Six is the number of empowerment. This is one of the most powerful and self-empowering paintings of the twelve. It will make a tremendous impact on the world, for everyone can identify with it.

Notice how the number six has been symbolized, remembering that three plus three equals six. There is a double trinity in it. Three is a very powerful number. It is the number of the Trinity — Father, Son and Holy Spirit. It is the number of the three angels that oversee these paintings, myself Michael, Gabriel, and Raphael.

There are two triangles. In other words, "two sets of three." One is where the roses come together, forming a triangle. Directly above that, the lines of light come together creating another. So the double triangles, with three sides each, vibrate with painting number six. The three red roses represent our Savior's blood shed for humanity and the passion of the cross. They also symbolize the Trinity.

I, as the divine archangel protector of the world, have a triangle engraved on my sword. My main mission on the earth plane is to protect all souls. I also rebuke evil, (not necessarily the nonbelievers, but evil). Evil can become an entity through negative thought forms. A triangle is a very powerful symbol, for it represents protection. Know that you will be guarded and safe when you breathe your last breath. For although there are trials and tribulations on the earth plane, and they will increase toward the close of this age, the year 2000, have no fear. I am the mighty archangel Michael, and I will herald you from one dimension into another.

The Resurrection

Mary's Message

You shall all rise to a Higher

Power — our Creator. The resurrection

of your souls is eternal. Have faith to know that

you shall rise victorious. You shall overcome the

earthly fear and rise to the heavenly love and peace

that you are promised. Blessings on souls who live in

faith, believing there is more beyond. There

is indescribable beauty, colors, grace,

and unimaginable divinity.

Believe, children, just believe.

Description of Painting

Christ rises glorious and immortal three days after His death. The essence of this painting looks angelic with gentle, soft pastel colors. Rays of light emanate from the face of Mary.

"The Banner of Victory" is a white banner with a red cross and is an emblem of the victorious, triumphant Christ. Banners are carried in processions to signify joy, victory, and triumph. Jesus is victorious over sin because He gave us the means of obtaining the remission of both original and actual sin. He also triumphed over death when by His own power He came forth from the tomb, proving thereby that He was stronger and superior to death."[7]

This is a painting of hope that we can all overcome our fear and rise victorious!

Background
Matthew 28:1-9

Now after the Sabbath, toward the dawn of the first day of the week, Mary Magdalene and the other Mary, the mother of James, went to see the sepulcher. And behold, there was a great earthquake; for an angel of the Lord descended from Heaven and came and rolled back the stone, and sat upon it. His appearance was like lightning, and his raiment white as snow. And for fear of him, the guards trembled and became like dead men. But the angel said to the women, "Do not be afraid; for I know that you seek Jesus who was crucified. He is not here; for He is risen, as He said. Come, see the place where He lay. Then go quickly and tell His disciples that He has risen from the dead, and behold, He is going before you to Galilee; there you will see Him. Lo, I have told you." So they departed quickly from the tomb with fear and great joy, and ran to tell His disciples. And behold, Jesus met them and said, "Hail!" and they came up and took hold of His feet and worshiped him.

Mary's Lesson

The painting, "The Resurrection," represents *faith and hope*. My Son rises victorious after three days in the tomb. He shows himself to me; He shows himself to others. One disciple does not believe; one is not sure. But nevertheless, My Son rose. He rose victorious. He rose triumphant. He overcame death as we know it. My Son is immortal. He is by my side. He has His throne in Heaven beside our Heavenly Father.

Faith is knowing that things will be fine when you can't see the answer to something. Faith is extending a hand to those who have hurt you, knowing that it is God's way, that it is a good and right thing to do. Faith is moving forward in your life through changes, through obstacles, knowing that it is not your power but God's power that works through you. Faith means being able to overcome things that might be holding you down on this earth plane — bad habits, destructive thoughts. Faith is a virtue.

Patience is learned through faith, because we wait when we have faith; we wait upon the Lord. Faith ennobles our hearts. Faith gives God the glory. Faith is persistent; it perseveres within itself.

I encourage you to have faith today. Faith starts as a mustard seed. Faith grows; faith flourishes. Be aware today of your faith.

Be aware of control issues within your life. When you control your life without the guidance of our Heavenly Father, then you are in a state of stress, confusion, and anxiety. To become whole with our Creator from whence we have come, we need to release faith.

Remember, we are all on an individual mission. Faith helps us get to the point where we know why we are here, what our mission is, what our purpose is. Our mission innately is to help humanity; to love humanity; to love ourselves; to give God the glory and the praise and the honor.

Hope casts out fear. Hope lets sunshine into every small darkened crevice. Hope is light. Hope enlightens the heart. Hope lifts burdens and makes us feel lighter and moves us closer to God.

Faith and hope are very important in your daily walk. My Son, Jesus, had faith to know that He would rise victorious. He had hope in His heart to know that He would sit next to His Father in Heaven, for He was told so.

I ask of you to read the Bible. There are tremendous insights in our Holy Bible — all truth, all that is good, all of it is the word of God. The holy word is contained in this book. Keep a Bible near you. Keep a Bible in your car. Read passages from the Bible daily. It will encourage you. It will give you hope.

We are all to be resurrected. When you take your last breath, your soul will rise to the heavens. I will wait for you, my precious children, each and every one of you. I will wait for you and my Son will be at my side.

Remember, the archangels are sent by me to protect and guide and love, for I am the Queen of Angels. Archangel Michael, I send to you as your protector, for he overcomes the evil one. He slays evil. He will be at my one side and my Son at the other, and we will meet you at the portal of Heaven.

Your soul will rise to us. The angels will sing, for there is great beauty in Heaven. Heaven is filled with light. Heaven is filled with beautiful music. Heaven is filled with beautiful colors. Heaven is peace. Heaven is love. Heaven is where God resides. He resides in our hearts. He resides in the air that we breathe. All that has been created, He resides in. God resides in Heaven; and you will be with the Holy Father — all in one and one in all — when you breathe your last breath — for your souls, my children, are eternal.

Remember, there is no beginning and no ending to your soul. There is no beginning and ending to God's compassion and love for you.

You should be filled with great joy for the revelation of the resurrection. The resurrection means that what my Son experienced was not in vain; that He had the faith to keep going, the faith to listen to His higher power, our Lord; the faith to overcome.

Now I give you all the banner of victory. Believe me, you will hold the banner of victory when you rise victorious into the heavenly realms. The banner of victory shows that you have overcome the world, that you have overcome the earthly plane of existence, to rise as my Son rose: victorious in the realms of light.

I ask you to pray for your heart to be opened to faith. Think about your faith. Think about God's love for you in response to your faith. He wishes so much for you to do His will, not your own will in a controlling way, but the will of our Heavenly Father.

"The Resurrection" means all that is beautiful, wonderful, blessed, divine, holy; all that is good, all that is spiritual. "The Resurrection" symbolizes the new dawning, the new spring.

Remember as we progress closer to the end of this age, we will be tempted, we will be tried, and sometimes we will be tested. We need to stand firm on solid ground. We need to rebuke what is evil. We need to do what is good.

Faith without good works is dead. Many of you have talents; many of you have special gifts. But without faith to know that these gifts will move forward toward a better humanity, these good works are dead. Good works without faith are also dead.

Remember in your daily walk to include faith. When my Son went through many towns healing the sick, uplifting the poor, their faith made them whole. Remember the woman who said to herself, "If I can just touch the hem of His garment, I will be healed." As He walked through the town, He felt the divine, healing energy from God go through Him and leave Him, and He turned and said, "Who touched me?" And He said to the woman, "Your faith has made you whole." It was her faith in knowing that all she had to do was a simple thing to be healed.

I am telling you, my children, it is not complicated. It is very simple. Heal yourselves. Ask for the Christ to come into your heart.

Have faith to know that you will be healed — healed of your physical ailments, healed of your emotional stress and anxiety.

You shall be healed, but you need faith to set the healing in motion. Read about faith in the Bible. Think of it as a virtue that must be instilled daily in your minds. You must draw in with faith, for you are loved and protected and watched over.

Please do not forget hope. Hope shows us the new day. Hope lets the shadows flee away. One way to understand the power of hope is to remember the seasons of the year. Autumn is beautiful, but it is a time of gentle dying. The leaves fall from the trees. Autumn is a time and a cycle of preparation. A preparation for retreat, for renewal, for rest, for reflection. Winter is that time of rest and reflection. Spring bursts forth with God's beauty. Spring is a time of rebirthing. Every year, we know that spring will be here. Every year, we watch our Master's hand in motion. I say to you, then, to think of the seasons. The summers of bounty, the falls of retreat, the winters of reflection, and the springs of hope and new beginnings, the springtimes of new dawning.

The Resurrection is like spring. Through the power of the Resurrection, we can start anew. We can be born from the earthly plane to the heavenly plane.

I encourage you now, as I hand you this banner of triumph, to take it and to hold it. Remember, you are on a crusade through this lifetime. Hold the banner proudly, knowing that you shall overcome. You shall overcome the world to a beautiful place — eternal, and peaceful.

Look on the painting, "The Resurrection," and remember, dear children, what I have said: Faith is the key to holding the banner of victory, and so is hope.

God bless each and every one of you. Blessings on your souls. God loves you.

Meditation

What joy it was to see my Son, Jesus, resurrected! We all shall rise eternally victorious in the love and light of God. We shall overcome the wiles of the world. We shall overcome all that has hurt us or those who have betrayed us. Trust the power of God within your hearts. Know that you are loved, my children. Your souls are eternal.

When my Son, the Christ, comes again, He will be carrying the *banner of victory*. It has a white background and red cross, and it symbolizes our ability to rise above what has held us down on this earth plane. Accept the banner of victory. Hold onto it in your daily trials and tribulations. Carry it with you in your mind and heart. Ponder the banner. It is symbolic of the greatest hope known to man — eternal life. You shall be resurrected in the Kingdom of God. God Bless all of your precious souls.

Sit quietly in a comfortable chair. Still your mind. Uncross your legs. Take several slow, deep breaths. Close your eyes. Take a few moments to be in God's Peace. Visualize a banner. This is your personal banner of victory. This banner will help you rise above obstacles in your life. Reach out and receive your banner and observe it. What colors or designs are on it? Is it heavy or light in weight? What shape or form is your banner? Now feel its triumphant power! Align your heart and mind with the Christ energy or consciousness. Remember to think of this symbol when you feel depressed, dejected, confused, and stressed. This symbol represents victory in all areas of your life.

The Resurrection Prayer

Hail Mary, full of grace, the Lord is with Thee!

Hail Lord Jesus, the Christ, our Savior, who is risen!

We praise You, Holy Heavenly Father,

for all that we have and all that we are.

There is hope to rise above adversity

and hope to soar with eagles.

We shall all rise as Christ —

victorious and ever in Your heavenly domain.

We have a Savior who calls us to look upward.

Look upward! Rise to the best of your abilities.

Rise to the power, glory, honor, and dominion that awaits you.

We shall see our Christ when He comes again,

carrying the banner of victory.

Let us, please, believe now in Him and all that is good.

We long to rise with our Savior

and long to be forever safe in the arms of You, O Mighty Lord.

We believe, we trust, we hope,

and we have undying faith in what is to come:

our personal victories!

Let us forever praise You in Your Kingdom, Lord,

resurrected and victorious.

Amen.

Archangel Gabriel speaks on "The Resurrection"

As the angel of resurrection, I help souls to resurrect, to rise glorious and victorious. Resurrection means faith to overcome obstacles on the earth plane and to rise gloriously, made anew, into the next realm or dimension.

Our Savior, the Christ, knew that there was life immortal. He knew that He would be in Heaven with His Father. He was told so. Therefore, He had faith and hope to know that He would endure being nailed to the rugged cross, and He would rise victorious. Through the shedding of His holy blood, all would be cleansed, purified, and become heirs to the throne of grace.

As the angel of resurrection it was I, Gabriel, at the tomb after the Sabbath, on Easter morning. I was sent to announce to Mary Magdalene, and Mary, the mother of James — that Christ was not there, for Christ had risen. I was sent because I am the divine messenger. "Do not be afraid," I said. "Jesus has risen."

As the angel of resurrection, I tell you to have faith to know that your soul is eternal and indestructible. You are sparks of the Divine Creator. No harm will ever come to your soul.

The face in this painting is quite angelic. The colors are very soft and pastel-like. They are very muted, and very, very gentle. Therefore, this delicate and angelic painting represents the light of hope and the power of faith.

Faith means walking forward — not by sight, nor by your own power, but by your belief. One might call it blind faith, but that's all right. Faith can move mountains. Faith can transcend anything that is unlike God. Please have faith. I, as Gabriel, admonish you to know that you will have life eternal. Christ rose after three days in the tomb, before His ascension. Then He walked on the earth to present Himself to some of His disciples, and even to some nonbelievers. He then ascended, but He is still among you. Christ is still in your hearts, in your minds. You need to remember the path of Christ. He was a gentle human being. The godhead was within him, for He is called the *Son of God*.

You are also heirs to the throne. You are sons and daughters of God. Therefore, what Christ can do, you can do also. People on the earth plane, at times, perceive the nine gifts of the Holy Spirit to be dead. The gifts of the spirit are very much alive! For great miracles of healing are happening now on the earth plane. There are great healings, for this is the time of cleansing and renewal. It's the time of resurrection. You need only to ask.

You now are in your earthly body, which is your hard shell, or shall I say your "cocoon." Yet, you all have a divine spark of the Creator within you, which is your soul. When you breathe your last breath, your soul leaves through the top of your head, rises above your body, and again, archangel Michael is there. I, Gabriel, the angel of resurrection, am also there to herald you into the next dimension, much as a butterfly leaves its cocoon. When you spread your soul wings and glide upon the realms of Heaven, you will rise free, timeless and eternally loved, into the Kingdom. This, dear ones, you must believe. For it is the truth; and I, Gabriel, am the messenger of truth.

There is a crescent moon in the upper right of "The Resurrection." The moon represents the lunar cycle which vibrates with the feminine. Mary is shown in many paintings throughout history as standing on the moon; one of our Blessed Mother's symbols is the crescent moon. There are crescent moons contained within many of the twelve paintings.

"The Resurrection" has beautiful, soft, golden yellows above Mary's head; and there is also the cross above Her head in all its glory. The cross, in this case, represents overcoming obstacles in the "crossroads of life." The upward diagonal strokes from Mary's shoulders also look like angel wings and represent wings to soar high above the earthly dimension.

I am very honored to oversee this painting. I dearly protect the painting of "The Resurrection," and I resonate and vibrate with its energy. Know that for humanity, indeed these paintings are very healing. These paintings were painted by the Blessed Mother's energy through Michele. Each one emanates a different feeling, a different soothing quality, and a different healing vibration. This healing vibration is to give you faith. It is to give you hope.

There are three crosses in this painting. Again, one is above Mary's head. Another cross is on the banner of victory, which is also flying on a cross. Three, as we have stated before, is the number of the Holy Trinity. These three crosses are very powerful.

The face in this painting is looking down at the banner of victory. This banner represents souls rising victorious. The colors in the banner are also very symbolic. White is the color of purity or cleansing. It is also the color of the divine spiritual. White pulls in angelic energy. Red represents the color of Christ's blood, shed for humanity. It also represents the physical plane of existence; because you, as human beings, are flesh and blood. Therefore, this banner represents the balance between the physical plane and the spiritual plane of existence. You are bound in the physical body of flesh and blood, but you will be resurrected to the spiritual realms of Heaven. The physical is contained within the spiritual in this case.

It is a very powerful meditation for you to take your personal banner, to hold it proudly and to know that you shall reign in Heaven with God — the Almighty, Mary, the angels, the archangels, and our Blessed Savior — the Christ. So I encourage you to think of your personal banner — whatever size, whatever color, whatever material. Hold onto it triumphantly. Have the faith and hope and hold the banner within your hearts. Know you shall overcome.

"The Resurrection" symbolizes enlightenment and rising again victorious. This painting was placed in the seventh position to show people that there are indeed new beginnings, new insights for every human soul, and the opportunity to rise again above evil and into God's love and light. Seven is the number of enlightenment. Christ rose from the tomb. He rose from the grave. He became one with the Creator. He now rules in the Kingdom of Heaven, as a mighty and gentle king.

The Lamb of God

Mary's Message

My Son, the Christ, took away the
sins of the world. You are all lambs, not to be
slaughtered but to be saved. God counts every one
of His beautiful and blessed children as His own
special ones. You are in the fold of grace. Forget
not that the almighty protection of God is unfailing.
My children, my lambs, you are loved always,
even until the close of the age and beyond.

Description of Painting

Christ is the Lamb of God who takes away the sins of the world. "The lamb is a symbol of Jesus, meek and humble of heart. It is a gentle, harmless animal; its voice soft and pleading. John the Baptist first called Jesus *Agnus Dei* — 'The Lamb of God.' This same expression is applied to Christ in certain holy ceremonies. Jesus was led to death (as the prophets foretold) like a lamb and did not resist or complain."[8] This portrayal means we are *one in the fold* of all that is. We are protected, unconditionally loved, and watched over by spirit.

The rays above the head of Mary represent our higher soul consciousness or our *oneness* with God. The white, eagle-like figure at upper right epitomizes strength to soar to great realms, and yet be in the gentle protection of God.

Background
John 1:24-30

They had been sent from the Pharisees, to Bethany beyond the Jordan, where John was baptizing. They asked John, "Then why are you baptizing, if you are neither the Christ, nor Elijah, nor the prophet?" John answered them, "I baptize with water; but among you stands one whom you do not know, even He who comes after me, the thong of whose sandal I am not worthy to untie."

The next day, he saw Jesus coming toward him, and said, "Behold, the Lamb of God, who takes away the sins of the world!" This is He of whom I said, "After me, comes a man who ranks before me, for He was before me."

Mary's Lesson

The painting, "The Lamb of God," symbolizes redemption. I come to you now to tell you that you are in the "fold of grace." My Son, the Good Shepherd, watches over you. He leads you on the good path.

Follow Him, my lambs. Follow my Son on the good path. He came into this world as the Lamb of God who takes away the sins of the world; who took away your sins so that you will enter our Divine Kingdom unblemished, untainted, and pure. My Son, the Lamb, gave His blood so that you might be saved.

I tell you now that you will all be saved — those who believe and follow my Son, for He is the Good Shepherd. You shall not want anything in the Kingdom of Heaven. He will make you lie down and have great peace. He will watch over your every step during this earthly life and forever more. My Son will be beside you, in front of you, behind you, above you, below you.

Remember, my Son is the Son of love, pure unconditional love from our Father. You are all lambs my children, all lambs; not to be slaughtered as my Son, because He was slaughtered for you. You are all lambs to be saved, to be redeemed.

I open my mantle, and I encourage you to come to me. Come to me, for I will intercede. I will take your prayers to Heaven. Put down your burdens. Put down your crosses. Be free. Be free to walk the good path. Be free from anything that is unlike God.

My Son was meek. He was humble, compassionate and true. He was true to Himself and true to His mission, and He was true to His Heavenly Father, God. He was true to humanity, for there is truth in the word of God. God's truth prevails. God's word prevails now and forever more.

If at times, dear children, you feel vulnerable and hurt like a meek lamb, remember that my Son's blood was shed to save you. It was shed to empower you — empower you with love — empower you so that you can rise victorious.

I ask of you to be baptized in the name of my Son, Jesus, and our Heavenly Father. Come into my fold. Come into my arms. I will extend my arms and protect you, and hold you to my bosom.

My son, the Christ, the Lamb, asks you to come to Him. He asks you to come into His fold, into His Kingdom.

I say to you that you have all been sent here by God to love, and you will return to God in love.

Remember the biblical story of John, upon seeing Christ and saying, "Behold the Lamb of God who takes away the sins of the world." For John's eyes were open and he was able to see the essence — the pure divine essence — of my Son. He knew within his heart that Christ was our Savior and Redeemer.

Now I ask you to walk as John walked. Receive Christ, knowing that He is the Lamb of God, that He has completely taken away any sin.

I ask you right now to come unto my Son. Ask for forgiveness — forgiveness of sins on a daily basis: "Lord, forgive me. And Lord, forgive others for they know not what they do."

I place a gentle, loving and beautiful, humble lamb in your hearts. Many feel hurt, many feel dejected, many feel as lambs being led on a thorny and rocky path. But I tell you the path is made smoother and easier when you are behind my Son, the Good Shepherd, for He will anoint your head with oil. Your cup will runneth over. The Good Shepherd, my Son, watches your every step. Remember, the story of the shepherd who left 99 lambs to find the one that was lost. Though you feel lost sometimes in your daily walk, remember that Christ is looking for you. He wants to find you. He wants to find you in His heart, and He wants to find Himself in your heart. Christ is always in your heart, of that you need to be aware.

I look over the world, and I see great turmoil. I see my children — some in starvation, some in pestilence, poverty, and ignorance. I pray to my Father for the pain to be released from my dear children; the pain of this earth plane. I have shed many tears for the abuses I have seen, for the ignorance that I have known. But I have hope for all humanity.

I have given humanity many signs and many wonders. I have tried to leave permanent signs for all to believe, for humanity needs signs. Humanity needs something tangible to see. That is one of the reasons these paintings were created. They will be similar to the stations of the cross. They will energize and balance each individual, the way he or she needs.

I will meet you dear children at the gates of Heaven. Do not lose hope. I have not lost hope for you. My Son, Jesus, has not lost hope for you, nor has our Divine Father. Remember to have hope.

It is time now to soar like the eagle; to look up to God, our Father; to release what is no longer for your highest good. The eagle is a symbol of strength. It is a symbol of overcoming adversity. It is a symbol of empowerment. If you feel like a lamb — if you feel bound, if you feel at times confused — remember that you are the lamb. But you are also the eagle, for in this painting, "The Lamb of God," I inspired an eagle soaring to the great realms of Heaven — an eagle representing strength, perseverance, and faith. An eagle is surefooted on the ground. An eagle also flies with swiftness and directness. He glides on the winds of time.

When Christ is in your heart, you will soar with the wings of an eagle. An eagle is mighty. Remember, you are capable of soaring to great realms, to great heights. All of you can achieve not only what you want in your life, but what the Lord wants for you. That is the most important thing to do: His will.

When you are in a state of faith and self-empowerment, when God and Christ are within you, and when you are aware of their presence, then faith enters. You have the ability to spread your wings and to soar.

My dear children, believe — just believe — that you are in the fold of God's grace and love, that you are protected by my mantle, and that I send you motherly divine love.

We love each and every one of you individually. Go in God's peace. Remember that you are not alone and that all is well. Blessings.

Meditation

The Lord is your Shepherd, you shall not want, you shall not lack. All is provided for you because you are in the fold of love. The Lord, the Christ and myself, Mary, acknowledge and love all of you individually. You are special, just as you are. You are loved unconditionally. The lamb is a gentle animal — meek and mild.

Christ loves, protects, guides, and cares for His flock. Would He not leave 99 sheep to go search for the one that is lost? Christ will provide for your needs. He is your Good Shepherd. You must look to Christ as your leader; you must follow His footsteps; you must trust His guidance. He will not leave you desolate. He will come to you. My children, my lambs, we are united together. Keep the Lamb of God in your mind as a symbol of protection and gentleness.

Be at peace with yourself. Put the cares of the day aside. Think of a pleasant experience that you have had, or think of someone you truly love. This will help you center and feel good in the moment. Sit straight and relax your shoulders. Close your eyes and breath in five slow, deep breaths. With your eyes closed, try to picture a lamb — meek and mild. Where is your lamb (in a meadow, farm, garden)? What is your lamb doing right now? Now, call this precious baby to you. Accept the lamb that I, Blessed Mother, give to you. Pick it up and hold it close. Feel its heart beating gently and feel its downy wool coat. Embrace the lamb and be gentle with it. The lamb is you — for you are a lamb of God! Love yourself unconditionally. Release the blocks and pain of your past. Forgive now, one by one, all who have hurt you. Take a few moments to do this. Love yourself, as you love your Creator, and as you love others. You are precious and unique. You are also protected, guarded, and guided by your Creator. Know this and be at peace.

The Lamb of God Prayer

Our Father, who art in Heaven,

we know that You are our mighty protection.

You lift us up on eagles' wings, and You guard our souls.

You sent Your beloved Son, Jesus, to be our Shepherd;

to guide and direct our path through this lifetime.

We are in Your grace, Father,

in Your arms and in the fold of love.

The path might be rocky, but we know Christ will give us surefooting.

When we feel as weak and confused lambs,

then show us our Shepherd, the Christ,

walking steadily ahead of us.

Let us feel the love and special protection

He gives to each and every one of us.

Our sins are forgiven and we are cleansed

in the Blood of the Lamb, our Savior.

Give us the gentle, meek, and humble spirit of the lamb

and the obedience to follow You and Your Son, Dear Lord.

Let us rest our weary hearts and minds in Your divine keeping.

We know we are loved — saved — and we thank You with open hearts.

Praise the Lord with all your might, for He will always direct your path.

Amen.

Archangel Michael on "The Lamb of God"

I oversee painting number eight, "The Lamb of God," because I am the mighty angel of protection. This is a very gentle painting as our Lady looks upon the lamb. (If you look above our Lady's head, in the horizontal clouds, you might even see the outline of a lamb kneeling there. Its head is facing towards the right.) The lamb is symbolic of human beings. It is symbolic of souls.

Our Lady loves your souls, all of which are in the fold of God's love. All are loved equally on the earth plane. You should be working together, living peacefully together, and striving together in unity. Many times you are at odds, one against the other. Hopefully, as you progress to the new millennium, you will be joining hands with each other.

Mary opens Her mantle and accepts you — Her lambs — unto Herself. So remember, God loves all human beings equally, as does our Savior, the Christ, and our beautiful Lady, Mary. The Blessed Mother does not discount those who turn their back on God, for there is always hope. She calls Her children "Her lambs," and so does our Savior, the Christ, who is the Good Shepherd.

I love to oversee this painting, "The Lamb of God." If individuals on the earth plane knew how they were guarded, uniquely loved, and protected, they would feel better about themselves and better about their lives, for not one event, thought, or inclination goes unnoticed from Almighty God.

Of the paintings I oversee or "vibrate" with, I must say that this opens my heart in different ways. Although I do not have a human heart, I have a beam of light within me which is called the

Source-bond. The Source-bond within angels is connected to our Creator. Through the thought forms of Almighty God, all the realms of energy were created — such as the mineral kingdom, plant kingdom, human species, animal kingdom, angels, and archangels. There are many, many, different kingdoms and dimensions around the earth.

I come with good words for humanity, to tell you that upon viewing this painting, you will feel as small children do, not vulnerable (in the sense of being preyed upon) but gentle, innocent, and hopeful. For as you know, children see the world through the "eyes of wonder." Children do not judge. Small children love unconditionally. They have great imaginations. They are filled with joy. They love to create. Children come into God's Kingdom first. Remember our Savior said, "Do not rebuke the children; have them come unto me." If you become as one of these, a child, you shall surely enter the Kingdom of Heaven.

Therefore, the lamb in this painting represent a precious child. A child needs to be guarded, nurtured, and watched over. As adults you tend to push back the inner child. The inner child heals the adult! Again, the inner child loves unconditionally. So it is important when you gaze upon "The Lamb of God" that you set your inner child free. Have fun! The inner child loves to play. The inner child is the ultimate joy bringer, not only to yourself, but to others.

There is a tenderness about this painting. It personifies the feminine, divine love of the world. Our Lady is for all people, for all nations, for all nationalities, for all religions, and denominations. She comes to you in pure divine gentle love. She respects and watches over each individual, and shows no partiality from one to the other, for She loves mankind equally.

This painting, above all the rest, will release your inner child. Pray in the name of our Lord, for my energy to protect you, as archangel Michael. You are in the fold of God's grace. I will come to you as a mighty warrior. I will help you fight your enemies. The protection I will give to you has to do with emotional issues and with energy fields. I am not here to kill, wound, hurt, or maim individuals. Remember, this is an "energy concept." I am here to protect those who call upon me as Michael; to guard their energy field or their aura, to protect them physically in their comings and goings, and to keep individuals from harming themselves. This is one of my main missions on the earth plane. I, archangel Michael, guard all souls who believe. I am also assigned to prevent accidents. I have a band of angels beneath me. When I say "beneath me," they are my helpers.

We also roam and travel throughout the globe trying to divert suicides. We have heralded millions of souls into the light, but there is also a "gray area" for those who choose suicide. For it is not wise for a human soul to go against the will of the Creator and abuse his own body or take his own life.

I also rebuke evil. Evil can become an entity because any negative emotion can take its own form; for example fear, apprehension, anger, revenge, cruelty. These are negative emotions that come from darkness. The darkness is the absence of love and light. I, Michael, fight off the darkness, so that an individual can have light and love around them — so they are shining as the sun.

Remember, the blinding light of angels and archangels, for we shine brighter than the sun. Our energy is highly evolved because we have never been human. We are not better than. Remember, as it says in the Bible, we are above humans, but not better than. We can not feel emotion, nor can we reason.

We only take orders from the Creator and were created specifically to do the things that we were created to do. Human beings have free choice and free will which is a gift from God. It is a beautiful gift, but through free will some human beings choose to be nonbelievers.

I was created to guard the souls of those who believe. For there are two sects or groups of people; it is very simple, it is not complicated. There are the believers, and there are the nonbelievers. The believers believe in themselves as divine creations of God. They believe that they are on earth for a purpose and a mission. They believe their soul is eternal and indestructible. They believe that they will rise from their body upon death and be immortal — ever in the company of the Christ — to stand before God and to see His face. Believers have hope; they believe in love. They believe in all good things, just as children do.

There is a book called *A Course in Miracles*, which was written by two nonbelievers. As they actually started to engage in the book, and write the book, they became believers. Sometimes, when you seek your mission, pray for your mission and do what is for your highest good, you come into the realm of believing in all things. Remember, faith is believing in all things, both seen and unseen. Yes, I, as archangel Michael, have seen many individuals on the earth plane who are nonbelievers. I will protect the ones that call upon the Lord for He will send me to the individuals who are believers. You are all loved equally, but remember, the path is yours.

I encourage individuals to read the 23rd Psalm. It is about our Savior, the Good Shepherd. He guides and gently leads you. He extends His shepherd's crook to pull you from harm — to guard you from getting bloody in the thorns of life.

I, Michael, work with the energy of the Christ. I also pull those that are believers away from harm. We, as angels, admonish you to believe! We are in every chapel and cathedral, and around any altar that is created. To pull the angelic energy in around you, create an altar somewhere in your home and burn a white pillar candle there. Have fresh flowers if you can; especially roses, for they are our Lady's flower and the fragrance is beautiful. Put power objects on your altar, for example a cross. It can be made of gold or any material, but have a cross on your altar. Also a bowl of distilled water will attract the energy of the angels to you. You might want to get a potpourri holder and burn different oils. Rose scent draws in angelic energy and so does lavender. You might want to have an image of the Christ, or an image of our Lady, or objects with angels on them. Angels rejoice when they see a believer. Remember, there are different levels of angels. Some angels are designed just to guard homes, and even physical objects, like cars. I am the chief of all the angels, so I oversee much. Again, we do not have free choice or free will. Therefore, we wait for assignments and requests from you for assistance.

The colors are very soothing in this painting. There is a beautiful sweep coming from behind our Lady's face and from behind the lamb. This represents eternal love, never beginning and never ending. For love is eternal. "The Lamb of God" personifies all that is gentle, loving, and protected. I guard this painting and my essence is in the painting. When you view this painting, you will feel mightily loved and protected through its gentle strokes of color.

There are many beautiful symbols in this painting. A visionary eagle is positioned in the upper right. This was painted to represent the ability to overcome or rise above obstacles in your lives. You have the might and strength to soar with eagle's wings. The true believer does not take no for an answer. The true believer has faith to soar with eagle's wings and to rise above obstacles. Whether it be physical maladies, pain, or mental abuses — release the past. Let the past go! Start every day anew. Being in the "fold of grace" means that no matter what you do as a believer, you are always guarded and protected. There is a beautiful heavenly realm that awaits all of humanity. Believe this!

"The Lamb of God" is placed in the eighth position and represents infinite love. Eight is a power number. If you turn eight on its side, you will see the empowering symbol of infinity. With this painting, you are reminded that you are infinitely in the fold of God's grace. You will always be His children. You will always be His lambs.

The Descent of the Holy Spirit

Mary's Message

*May the dove of peace descend
upon your hearts. This is a time of great fear
and unrest. The dove of peace brings hope. Look up
and know the time is at hand. Open your spirits and
receive. Receive what your Heavenly Father wants so
much to give you. May God's grace fall upon you.
May His wisdom and knowledge entreat you,
and may you know He is the Way,
the Truth, and the Light.*

Description of Painting

After Christ's resurrection the Holy Spirit descended upon
Mary and the apostles. In this piece of artwork, the dove portrayed
at the top, represents the Holy Spirit and signifies our merging or
oneness with the Source — our Creator. "As the dove is a clean
and peaceful bird, so is the Holy Ghost the spirit of peace, holiness

and love."[9] The rays of light emanating from this bird signify the gifts and graces of the Holy Ghost and represent the *universal flow* or God's divine will for our lives.

The teal color used throughout the painting is to enhance the viewer's inward calmness, peace, and spiritual healing.

Background

Acts 2:1-4

When the day of the Pentecost had come, Mary and the apostles were all together in one place and suddenly a sound came from Heaven like the rush of a mighty wind, and it filled all the houses where they were sitting. And there appeared to them tongues as of fire, distributed and resting on each one of them. And they were all filled with the Holy Spirit and began to speak in other tongues, as the spirit gave them utterance.

Mary's Lesson

The painting, "The Descent of the Holy Spirit," means *gifts of the spirit*. I bring to you the dove — the dove of purity, of gentleness. The dove represents the Holy Spirit, the Trinity.

Many doves have descended to the earth plane. Many doves of peace have entered many hearts, for you need peace now in your lives. You need inner peace.

God gives you His peace. My Son, the Christ, gives you His peace. I give you my peace.

Let not your hearts be troubled, neither let them be afraid. This is a time of great unrest, as we reach the upcoming decade; but I tell you that through the power of prayer you can raise the vibration of this earth plane. Every thought, every prayer is acknowledged by me personally and by our Creator.

I encourage you to form prayer groups. When two or three or more are gathered in my Son's name, He is in the midst of them. Make it a point to attend a prayer group or to start a prayer group in your home. Sit in a circle, hold hands, visualize my Son in the middle of you. Pray for the sick. Pray for the needy. Pray for each other — for each other's healing. Pray for the wisdom and the divine knowledge of the Lord to be upon you. When I was with the apostles and the Holy Spirit descended upon us, it was like tongues of fire.

There are many, many gifts of the spirit. *Discernment* is given to those with spiritual gifts, so that they can use them wisely. My Son had all the gifts of the spirit, and you are heirs to our throne. When you walk my Son's path, the path of our Father, you will receive gifts.

God has already given you a precious gift — free choice and free will. I ask you now to make a decision; now is the time for decision making. Choose now which path you want to walk. Free will is to do the Creator's will — to choose to serve the Creator, to choose to praise the Creator — to choose to accept God's truth in your heart.

All need peace now, in this time of great unrest. I suggest praying daily, meditating daily. Think of the white dove of peace. Put that dove into your heart. Ponder the power of the Holy Spirit and the Blessed Trinity — the Father, the Son, the Holy Spirit.

All gifts are from God. They come and fall upon you like a gentle rain of rose petals from Heaven. I want to shower you, my children, with blessings. Let the rain of rose petals, which symbolize blessings, fall around you and fall into your heart and mind.

There is a difference between prayer and meditation. When you meditate, you center yourselves. You go inward. Prayer is the reaching out and the extending outward to our Heavenly Father — extending your praise, extending your gratitude, extending your love back to Him. Again, meditation is going within. Meditation means listening to what our Heavenly Father wants to say to you. It is that still inner voice that is synonymous with God's voice. It is the voice of your soul. It is the voice of the Lord, for you were created from our Lord.

I ask you to spend an hour each day, in the morning or in the evening, communing with our Lord — listening, listening, listening. You might want to walk in nature as you pray.

Again, block off at least an hour for prayer and meditation time daily. Thank the Creator for everything He has given you. Remember to remain in humble gratitude. Thank Him for your life, for your soul, for all that is around you, for your opportunity to be here on the earth plane. Thank Him for sending my Son in human form so that you might have abundant and eternal life and be forgiven of all that you have done. Then pray for help. Pray for the help of humanity, for the homeless and needy. Pray for souls to come into the light — into the light of our Father in Heaven, into His divine, pure, white light. Ask for help in your own lives daily, for you need to see what is true, pure, good, and holy.

Remain in gratitude, ask for help, and remember to listen. This is where the meditation will come to you. The listening is very important. Listen to your heart. Listen to the promptings of what God wants to give you.

By renewing your spirit and your energies, it will help you to be an open vessel, an open channel through which God's love flows. When you have peace in your hearts, you are calm and serene within yourselves, and then you are able to reach out and give that peace to others.

God wants you to have peace. I pray for each and every soul that the power of the Holy Spirit falls upon each head; that the power of the Holy Spirit enters each heart; that you receive all the gifts of the spirit.

Remember to read the Bible. In First Corinthians the gifts of the spirit are mentioned. Read the New Testament — about my Son and His life and His works. Read about the power of the Holy Spirit. Your lives, my children, are not in vain, for you are all here to do good works.

Think about peaceful colors on your nature walks. Think about healing colors: rose, blue-green, soft purples. I give you healing by the power of my Father in Heaven, and the power of my Son, and all of the saints. I wish for you healing in your life. I wish for you to be healed in the name of my Son, Jesus.

This is a great time of healing. Humankind has destroyed lands through pollution and through self-centered motives, but there is a wave of healing happening now. Have peace to know that this healing will occur. You are being rained upon with beautiful signs from our Creator; you will never be alone.

May the dove of peace alight upon you. Accept your Holy Call, each and every one of you. Accept what God has in store for you. Open up. I send you blessings, my children, now and evermore.

Meditation

May the dove of peace descend upon you. May you receive all the gifts of the spirit. Our Creator has given you many gifts; the greatest is the gift of life and free choice. By receiving free choice, you decide whom to serve. Obedience, patience, trust, and faith are asked of you. Through choosing to serve our Lord and His Son, Christ, you walk the path of hope, love, and eternal life. Serving may mean sacrifice as you draw ever closer to the truth. The truth is the word of God. The Bible represents this great truth. Please read the words of God and remember them. You cannot serve two masters. You cannot serve God and man! Choose the way of truth and peace.

I give you this dove of peace to put into your hearts. Carry the dove with you. Know that in future times, peace within is most important. There can only be true peace from within. Many answers lie within ourselves. Think of the white dove — pure and holy. Think of the meaning of this beautiful bird of peace.

Sit quietly in a comfortable position. Relax your body starting with the feet. Be aware of a relaxing sensation — starting at your feet, moving up through your ankles, calves, thighs, abdomen. Take several deep breaths. Continue to let the relaxation flow up through your chest region, throat, and face. Relax now all the muscles of your face, and now the top of your head. Close your eyes. Empty your mind. See a beautiful white dove. This is the dove of peace I give to you now. See the gentleness of its demeanor. Put the dove symbolically into your heart. How do you feel? Know that you can carry the dove of peace within you. Know now that in future times, peace for yourself is most important. True peace comes from within. Think again of the white dove — pure and holy. Now ponder global peace — envisioning this dove covering our world with its wings of protection. Hear the gentle cooing of its song, see the elegance of its flight and appreciate the regalness of its stance. May this dove remain among you and in you, until you stand before our Creator and see the Face of God.

The Descent of the Holy Spirit Prayer

Dear Lord,

We know the best prayer is the simplest!

We pray for peace.

Peace in our hearts, our nation, and the world.

Let Your dove of the Holy Spirit descend upon our lives

in gentleness and peace.

We accept the purity and beauty of the dove.

We receive You, Father, and the Christ in our lives.

Come, O Holy Dove, and enter within!

Let us feel tranquil and serene each day of our lives.

Help us to know that true peace.

The peace of God starts within.

Let us spread peace

throughout our neighborhoods, states, and nations.

Help us to teach our children respect

for all living things and for the property of others.

We feel the power of Your spirit, dear Lord, in us and among us.

Help us also to have discernment

to know what the gifts of the spirit truly are.

We are bathed in gentle light from above.

Dear Heavenly Father, we thank You now and forever for Your peace!

Amen.

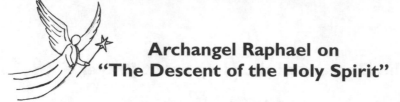

Archangel Raphael on
"The Descent of the Holy Spirit"

Painting number nine, entitled "The Descent of the Holy Spirit," represents the nine gifts of the Holy Spirit, which are mentioned in the Bible, 1 Corinthians 12:4-11.

Our Savior, the Christ Jesus, possessed all these gifts. I, Raphael, oversee these special gifts. Know that these gifts are alive today. For Christ said, "You can do as I do, and greater things than I shall you do." Therefore, remember the gifts of the spirit are available to all of you. The gifts of the Holy Spirit are a sovereign manifestation of the Lord and are given only as the spirit wills.

The first gift is the *word of wisdom*. This comes upon individuals so that they may speak the truth. They may speak words of wisdom from the Lord. They do this to help humanity to come to the light, and to come to the truth.

The second spiritual gift is the *word of knowledge*. This knowledge comes over an individual, and they can hear the Lord's voice, whether it be audible or whether it be a knowing in their heart. Many spiritual healers today use the word of knowledge. For example, they will receive a word from our Lord about a pain in a person's body, or what a person can take nutritionally to help themselves.

Faith — the third gift — can move mountains. There are many faith leaders in the world. These individuals help humanity persevere toward your mark, toward the goal of walking a Christ-like path, and eventually, of course, communing with our Heavenly Father, eternally forgiven in the realms of grace.

The fourth spiritual gift is the *anointing of healing*. Through the power of the Holy Spirit, people are made well in all parts of their body by the "laying on of hands." When an individual has the anointing of healing, his hands get very warm and sometimes feel "on fire." This indicates that a person near him needs healing. Along with this gift, the word of knowledge is usually used to define what part of the body needs healing. Again, this word can come from an audible voice from God, a *knowing*, or sometimes an actual "fleeting pain" in the anointed one's body. When hands are laid on the sick individual, the power of the Holy Spirit moves through those hands (like a feeling of heat or fire) into the diseased part of the body. At that point the person is totally healed.

The *working of miracles* is the fifth gift of the spirit. This encompasses everything that would be considered a miracle. Not just healing miracles, but miracles in other areas of humanities needs. For example, in the Bible, Jesus' first miracle was at the wedding at Cana where He turned the water into wine. There was also the miracle of the fish and loaves multiplying to feed the hungry masses, when Jesus taught near the Sea of Tiberias. The working of miracles can be done in your own lives through prayer. Blessed Mother Mary says wars can be averted, and world peace can be achieved through prayer. Many of you have experienced physical, emotional, and financial miracles through prayer! Miracles are gifts and prayer is the catalyst.

Prophecy is another gift of the spirit. It is being able to see around an individual, to gently guide them to where they need to be, and to tell them that which is for their highest good. There were many prophets in the Bible — Daniel, Ezekiel, Isaiah, Moses, Elijah, and John the Baptist to name a few. Today prophets may speak of things like global earth changes, ascension into Heaven, and energy shifts and patterns. The gift is used to enlighten, encourage, and ennoble your fellow man.

Discernment of spirits, or the ability to distinguish spirits, is another gift that is very important. This is *knowing* which individuals are for your highest good and which individuals are telling you the truth. It is also knowing which situations to enter into and which to avoid. Discernment is one of the most important spiritual gifts, especially when it is used with other spiritual gifts. It is the "gift of protection." In healing, an individual with this gift can also detect "spirits" — of depression, suicide, drug addiction, alcoholism — which are created through the inflicted person's fear and anger. Through the power of the Holy Spirit, these negative spirits are removed with the anointing of healing.

The eighth gift is *speaking in tongues*. When the power of the Holy Spirit comes upon you, you are able to speak of things of which you have no knowledge. The spirit, who is mightier than you, speaks through you. You become a channel for divine knowledge. Remember, when the Blessed Mother and the apostles were together praying after the passing of the Christ, the heavens opened up. The gifts of the spirit fell upon them like tongues of fire at each shoulder; and they started to speak in tongues for they were filled with the power of the Holy Spirit. Speaking in tongues is a universal prayer language with God.

The last spiritual gift is the *interpretation of tongues*. By the power of the Holy Spirit, you will know what was said and be able to interpret what was said. This knowledge or interpretation, can be for yourself or others. When you speak in tongues it is like speaking in a strange language. You don't know what you are saying to God, until God gives you the interpretation.

The biblical gifts of the spirit are important; but because I am an angel of virtues, I am here to remind you that virtues are also important. Virtues are the commendable traits and talents that an individual possesses. Remember your talents. Some have artistic talent; others have physical ability for athletics; some are good gardeners or cooks, and some work well with their hands. Also leadership abilities and smiles are gifts, just as being loving, generous, and kind are important gifts. Patience is a virtue, but also a gift; humility is the same.

If you would like to know what your spiritual gifts are, or how you can develop them, pray in the power of our Heavenly Father, and in the name of Christ, and your gifts will be revealed to you. Whatever you love to do for humanity's good is a spiritual gift. For example, take a blank sheet of paper and list five things that you "love to do." These things are synonymous with your soul's purpose and also your talents or gifts. Try to do more of the things you love each day.

This painting, "The Descent of the Holy Spirit," is very calming. The colors are predominately blue and green, with various shades of teal. In the center top of the painting is the most beautiful dove, which represents the embodiment of the spiritual gifts. Let the clouds part in your life. Let the shadows flee away. Look up, and you will see the holy dove of peace, containing the power of the Holy Spirit. Let it descend upon you as it did when Christ was baptized, and as it does today in every heart.

Mary has a serene look on Her face as the power of the Holy Spirit is descending upon Her, bringing Her also the gifts of the spirit. There is a gentle flow around the face of Mary, and underneath Her. The ocean is shown at the bottom portion of the painting. This represents your soul-conscious mind, that ever connects you with the Source — your higher power — which is God, the Creator.

"The Descent of the Holy Spirit" represents not only the gifts of the spirit, but the power behind the spirit. This is not the power to control yourselves or the masses, but true self-empowerment which comes from knowing that you are divine sparks of the Creator, and that the Divinity is within — the "I am" presence.

I, Raphael, will encourage you as an individual in any creative pursuit that you desire. Through your gifts and talents, and through sharing them with others, you heal the world. For the world is hungry for knowledge. It is hungry for prophecy, for good deeds, good thoughts, and healing. The world wants to know that it is loved. Individuals on the earth plane want to know that they are protected by a divine presence. Therefore, for each and every individual that gazes upon this painting, I wish that their heart opens up and that they let the power of the Holy Spirit enter within.

Enter within o' dove of peace! Enter within the power of the Holy Spirit. Praise the Lord all ye many souls on the earth plane. For gifts are as alive today as they were in biblical times. This is known to be true. For God is the same yesterday, today, and forever. God is eternal. He changes not. He created you and the world, and He is pleased with His handiwork. Therefore, honor your God all the days of your life. Seek the gifts of the spirit. Start where you are, at the place where you are. Reach out and touch someone today. Be ever hopeful. Stay in your faith. Be discerning with that which is around you. Know that you are loved. May peace be among you and remain in your hearts.

This painting was placed in the ninth position in the series of twelve, because it resonates with the nine spiritual gifts in the

Bible. Nine vibrates with humans engaging in divine gifts or those seeking their own spiritual gifts. Number nine is a very high vibrational number. It connects us with the divine within, but also connects us with our own awareness and our own talents. That is why this painting is placed in the ninth position.

Gifts come in many forms. They are not limited to great talent. They call only for you to do that which you are best at doing, and to do it with all your might. It may be a smile, a hug, a prayer, a touch; working efficiently with hands through cooking, gardening, or even flower arranging. The list may go on and on. Every good and perfect gift is from God, our Heavenly Father — the Father of Lights.

The Assumption

Mary's Message

As I was raptured into Heaven to
sit at the throne of grace beside my Son,
so shall all of you who believe be with us. You
are heirs to the throne. Majestic beauty awaits
you. Please do not close your hearts. I am the Star
of the Sea. Follow my Son and me to glory and
victory. The waters of life may toss and rock you,
but God is your foundation. I will help the lost
and intercede for all who pray. There is power
in prayer, my precious ones.

Description of Painting

The tenth painting personifies the Blessed Mother being raptured
into Heaven and united with Her Divine Son. We also are now in
the process of being raptured into perfect harmony and oneness
with the Creative Source, our Maker.

The circular *sunbow* around Mary's face represents hope,
peace, and promise. The three roses are symbolic of the Trinity
and stand for Mary's essence: sweetness and light. Clockwise from

top, the fuchsia rose symbolizes divine protection; the white and yellow rose, purity of purpose and spiritual wisdom; and the delicate pink rose, unconditional love.

This is a painting of heavenly, divine bliss and eternal tranquility. The rising waves at the bottom seem to push us ever higher, merging us with the universal life flow — the godhead.

Background

Luke 1:46-55

Then Mary said, "My being proclaims the greatness of the Lord, my spirit finds joy in God, my Savior, for He has looked upon His servant in Her lowliness; all ages to come shall call me blessed. God who is mighty has done great things for me, holy is His name; His mercy is from age to age on those who fear Him. He has shown might with His arm; He has confused the proud in their inmost thoughts. He has put down the mighty from their thrones and raised the lowly to high places. Since we believe that Jesus died and rose again, even so, through Jesus, God will bring with Him those who have fallen asleep...and so we shall always be with the Lord."

"The Assumption was a real event about which we should have no doubt; rather we should have for it in our faithful hearts certainty, joy, hope, seeking to understand the symbolic value which this miraculous fact holds in the economy of salvation and in Christian behavior,"said Pope Paul VI. "The Assumption is the triumph not only of the most pure soul of Her who was blessed among women, but likewise of Her innocent, virginal, and immaculate body. May our Lady assumed into Heaven hold us to relish physical purity and spiritual beauty."[10]

Mary's Lesson

I, Mary, the Blessed Mother, was raptured bodily into Heaven to sit at the throne of grace with my Father and my Son, Jesus. All of you will join us, all who believe, for you were conceived in love. You were created from our Divine Father to live in harmony and peace among the earth plane.

I come to you at this time of unrest to say that there is great hope for all of humanity. Each one of you counts one to the other, so be kind to one another. Be gentle with yourselves.

The heavenly realms are beautiful. They are filled with great light, color, and peace. Reach out and accept the heavenly realms into your heart now.

The painting, "The Assumption," represents *devotion to Mary*. This painting calls for devotion to me because I come as a spokesperson for my Son, the Christ, and for our Heavenly Father.

You need to be devoted to our Heavenly Father first, from whence you have come and into whose bosom you shall return. Our Heavenly Father created you, loves you, and wants you to be whole. You must pray to the Father first and always. He is all powerful and all knowing, and surrounds you each day with gentle love. We must also pray in the name of my Son, Jesus Christ. There is tremendous healing power in prayer.

I come to you with the feminine, divine spirit of love, healing, joy, and abundance. I ask you to become balanced in your daily walk, and balanced in all areas of your life. Align yourselves with what is good.

I am your friend. I am your Mother. I am your divine intercessor. I will take your prayers to Heaven. It was a glorious day for me when I was able to stand at the feet of my Heavenly Father in the throne room of grace. Remember, you are all children. If you have not had a happy childhood — if you have been abused, hurt or wounded — remember, you can take that hurt to our Heavenly Father, who wants so much for you to be whole, balanced, aligned, and in perfect harmony — one to the other.

I ask you now to pray. Pray in the name of my Son, Jesus Christ. Pray to our Heavenly Father, for He knows the needs of each and every one of you; and remember, He knows your thoughts and prayers before they are heard.

Also remember that prayer and meditation time means communion with our Father. He wants you to come to Him as children asking forgiveness in all humility, remaining patient in your daily walk and steadfast to the truth.

The truth is the word of our Father, the word of God. The truth shall set you free. Put your cares, your worries, and your problems on God's altar; He will cleanse each and every one of you. He will cleanse your sins.

My Son came to this earthly plane in the form of a human being, a Son of God, so that you could relate to God from whence you have come. God is in everything beautiful, in everything good. God knew that humanity needed a physical human being to relate to, and so the beautiful, transitional idea of creating a human son was conceived.

My Son, Jesus, walked a hard and rocky path, but He had faith in His heart — faith to know that He would have life eternal, and so shall all of you. You shall rise victorious and be ever-resurrected, reborn eternally to be with our Father; for in His house are many mansions; and He is preparing a place for all of you to come and be with Him.

Pray the Lord's Prayer. Pray the 23rd Psalm, for the Lord and my Son are your shepherd. You shall want for nothing in His

Kingdom. You are here to have life fully on the earth plane, and you are here to have it more abundantly. Remember to love your neighbor as yourself. Remember to be kind to strangers.

I am manifesting more and more towards the end of this century and the dawning of the new millennium, because my people, our people, need hope. By sending prayers daily, you empower the good. By thinking in fear, worry, or anger, you weaken the link to our Heavenly Father and you weaken the unifying link to all the world.

I bring you joy. I bring you hope. Know that Heaven is beautiful and peaceful. You shall all be resurrected and you shall all overcome death. Death is a passing from one form to another. Death leaves the physical body behind, but the soul is eternal and indestructible. Your soul is truly you. Your soul is God's breath of life.

We shall rapture your souls to Heaven, as I was raptured to Heaven. There will be a new ascension. My Son, the Christ, is returning in glory, in honor.

You need to praise the Lord. You need to praise my Son. It is not about praying to the angels or praying to me. Communion is about praying to our Father, in the name of my Son, Jesus Christ, for our Father is the source of all.

I am only the humble intercessor. By being devoted to me, you have allegiance with me, and you become an ally.

I love you all. You are my friends, my children. I tell you that to align yourself with me is to align yourself with my Son and our Father.

Devotion is a wonderful thing. It is like love. It is good to be devoted to the cause of Christianity, and it is good to be devoted to the beauty that awaits you. I will always be around my children, sending nurturing love and care their way.

Remember to be devoted in your prayer time. Be devoted to the word of God. Be devoted to meditation time, to helping others, to giving of yourselves.

Remember to be devoted also to bringing love back to yourself, for your body is the temple of God. Your body is the temple of the Holy Spirit. Your body houses your soul. Take care of yourselves, my children. Take care of your physical bodies by exercising, walking, deep breathing, and stretching. Take care of your mental capacities by meditating, reflecting, retreating, and relaxing. Take care of your spiritual development by staying in your prayer time and learning what God has for you. Read the Bible. The Bible is the true word.

I love you all, and I am here to bring hope now to these troubled times, for your path on the earth plane is not an easy one. Our children need love. Our children need to be shown the way. You can be missionaries in your daily walk by smiles, good thoughts, and good deeds. But remember, our children are our future and our hope.

I tell you there will be three days of darkness on the earth plane at the end time. We need to prepare for this. This will be coming fairly soon. I only tell you, not to instill fear within you, but for you to prepare. Prepare yourselves with the armor of light which is God's word. Prepare yourselves by being devoted in your prayer time, by having faith to know that you shall rise above the earthly plane to the heavenly realms to be with us eternally loved, and in peace and in joy. As I was assumed into Heaven, so shall all of you be.

You need to balance and align by getting good nutrition into your bodies. Remember that your temple must be nourished. Drink plenty of distilled water. Eat organically grown, dark green, leafy vegetables, fruits, and whole grains. Try to refine your lifestyles. Try to show yourselves self-discipline.

Remain joyful as a child. Let your inner children out to play, to relax and to share life abundantly. Your inner child will heal you, because your inner child believes all. Unless you become as children, you can not enter our Kingdom. This does not mean in folly or games, but it means in unconditional love. We must bring out the inner child that loves unconditionally, that believes, that sees the truth, that is not afraid to speak the truth. Children always speak the truth.

Think back to the ages of one to five. These are the formative years in our world, when children speak their truth. They see our heavenly realm and our angelic realm. They laugh; they love. When my Son said, "Send the children to me; turn them not away," He saw them as individual souls. He brought them into His fold, His arms of love. So I encourage you to try to be more childlike, to try to see the world through the eyes of your inner child — your beautiful, precious, inner child.

Remember, there is vast glory, majesty, and splendor that await all of you.

I am asking you to be devoted to me, because it will help you balance and align, for I shall intercede and take your prayers to our Heavenly Father. Be devoted to the feminine, divine, healing love. Be devoted to nurturing, to opening your hearts in a warm way towards each other.

Align yourself with me, my Son, and our Father. I ask this all of you, for there is not much time left. Daily ask for forgiveness. This is the way through Heaven's gate. Forgive others who have hurt you.

Remember to stand firm in your beliefs in the word of God. I shall see you all, and shall touch every hand and heart when the rapture begins, when my Son descends for you and takes you with Him to glory.

God's grace be upon you. May His peace entreat you. May you know the Way, the Truth, and the Light.

Meditation

The time is soon coming for you to be raptured into the next dimension — Heaven. Beautiful music, colors, and light of indescribable magnitude await you. In the blink of an eye you will be taken, when my Son returns. The *sunbow* symbolizes hope that you will rise with our Savior and forever be in the Kingdom of bliss. The sunbow represents alignment — all the colors manifesting together in a single form. We need to prepare for what is to come. It is important, children, to pray and say the rosary. Think deeply of the life of your Savior and ponder the importance of His life here on earth. Pray for world peace — for the abused children and animals. Animals are God's creation, and He loves them so.

I give you the sunbow. There will be more seen as we reach closer to the time of ascension. Look up and see the prisms in the sky! I send you sunbows as a sign of promise. When you see one think of the Divinity to come. Hold this prism of light in your mind. Meditate on your alignment — your physical, emotional, mental, and spiritual perfection — as you reach up closer to the Kingdom of Heaven.

You are now sitting and relaxing. Roll your shoulders back several times. Then lower them, releasing all tension and worry. Take eight slow, deep breaths. Slowly close your eyes. Put your hands, with palms facing up, on your lap. Remain still. See, in your mind, the beautiful blue sky. In the distance is a sunbow or prism of light. What shape is your sunbow? See it glisten and sparkle. It is moving closer to you. It is now over your head. Feel its aligning power! Now, hold this prism of light in your mind. Meditate for awhile on your personal alignment. First your physical body. If there is any pain, release it, for you no longer need the pain. Align your emotional state by now releasing fear, anger, and negativity. Replace it with love, peace, and joy. Now align your mental processes. Cast out confusion and troubled ways of thinking. Replace them with positive and uplifting thoughts. Align yourself spiritually now by thinking of our wonderful and loving Creator, who created your divine soul eons ago. For your soul is eternal and indestructible. The sunbow will always balance you. Look to the skies. There will be many actual sunbows appearing as we reach closer to the ascension! When you see one think of the Divinity to come.

The Assumption Prayer

We know, O Most Loving Father,

that Mary, the Mother of Your Son, was raptured into Heaven.

There She rules with gentle grace and humility.

Let us know that we too shall be raptured at the end time

to receive what is ours in Heaven.

Let us believe and know that Mary and Jesus wait for us,

and that we are never alone.

We believe in the beauty and magnitude of Heaven.

We believe in joy and eternal happiness that awaits us.

Let us now heed the call for a good life with good works and deeds.

Let us strive upward reaching toward Heaven

and always keeping in our prayer time.

We pray for world peace

and that all souls will be raptured to a better, beautiful, and divine place.

We know this and believe.

We accept Your promise, Dear Lord, and Your Holy Word!

Thank you for listening to our prayers.

Amen.

Archangel Gabriel on "The Assumption"

I guard over this painting because one of my missions is actually to guard over Heaven. "The Assumption," painting number ten, symbolizes Mary's Assumption into Heaven.

Mary was assumed body, mind, and soul into Heaven. I came to Her as Gabriel, and I wrapped my mighty large wings of protection around Her and enveloped Her. There was an immediate connection, for She knew after She was crowned that She would be "Queen of the Angels." She felt safe and protected as we entered the heavenly Kingdom. And what a glorious day it was! There was great rejoicing, great joy, and happiness. She entered the throne room looking as a peasant woman. Then She was clad with purple velvet robes, and the golden crown was placed on Her head.

All the angels sang. There was a beautiful choir of harmony that rose from the heavens as never before. And yes, there are even cherubs in Heaven as you would call them — baby angels. They attend our Blessed Mother constantly, because She loves children and babies.

Mary was assumed or raptured into Heaven, and the earth plane will never be the same! Her earthly body was instantly raptured into the heavenly Kingdom. She then started over in Her soul body in the heavenly realm. When Mary was assumed into Heaven, Her earthly mission was complete. Now She reigns as the Queen of Peace, the Star of the Sea, the Lily of the Valley, the Bright Morning Star, our Beloved Lady of Grace, the Mystical Rose — for She has been given many names and titles.

This painting shows a glimpse of the heavenly Kingdom.

Notice the circular sunbow. We call it a sunbow because there is no rain in Heaven; nor is there any darkness or nighttime, but there are beautiful prismatic colors. You, as human beings, are walking prisms. You vibrate with prismatic color on the earth plane and also in the heavenly realms. The sunbow starts at the back of Mary's head, moves from left to right around the front of Her, and ends under Her chin. This oval or circular shape is a symbol of completion and eternal love.

The sunbow, in this case, also represents aligning and balancing all areas of your lives. For when the prism shines, all the colors are balanced beside each other. This is an empowering painting, and as you look at it you will feel more balanced in the areas you need to be. The *sunbow of completion* calls for you to be balanced in all areas — physically, mentally, emotionally, and spiritually. I admonish you to complete tasks in your life, and be aware of balancing your time, energy, and efforts for a common goal.

This is one of the most colorful of all of the twelve paintings. Every shade of the rainbow is included in this painting. Again, the crescent moon is shown under the sunbow representing the feminine, divine, healing essence which Mary portrays. In the upper left corner is the sun, representing the masculine energy. So, contained in this painting, we have a balance between the masculine and feminine. I, archangel Gabriel, am here to announce to you that you shall be balanced in all areas of your life; your feminine side shall be balanced with your masculine side.

There are three mystical roses of the most beautiful shades and hues. These roses also represent balance, because they symbolize the physical plane, the spiritual plane, and the emotional plane of existence.

The top rose on the upper right represents the blood that Christ shed. It also represents the passion of Christ and the passion in our lives to produce what is of the highest good. It is the rose of creativity; therefore, I ask you to find things that you love to do and create them with all your might, from the wellsprings of love in your heart. For this is a rose of encouragement. It encourages you to move forward in creative directions and to share all the talents and love that you have with humanity.

Next there is the white rose with the golden center, which is the light of God. It is balanced between the rose of encouragement for creative pursuits and passion, and the pale pink rose representing pure, unconditional love. The white rose symbolizes spirituality, cleansing, and purification. Your spirituality and awareness are very important in your daily walk. Believe in the Divine. Believe that you will be among the heavenly realms with all of us. So when you gaze upon the white rose with the golden center, think about the ability to soar to new heights, to complete tasks, to balance all areas of your life.

Again, the pale pink rose next to Mary's face means unconditional love and the emotional plane of existence, for heart love is contained here. Rose is Blessed Mother's favorite color, and remember, She is called the divine Mystical Rose. Her heart opens and exudes great fragrance of love for humanity, for Her children. Therefore, this rose is closest to Her own heart in the painting. When you gaze on the three beautiful roses, you will feel a new divine inner peace and balance.

This is a highly symbolic painting and a very mystical one. Note the waves rising on the lower left corner. This expresses the soul-mind consciousness, in other words, your own divinity with the working of the Divine Creator. It lifts you ever up and moves you ever forward on your spiritual development and journey. Rise to the best of your abilities. Let the cosmic waters of life push you up and out towards all that is divine and good. Give all the talents and love that you have to humanity.

Above Mary's head is a dash of purple, and also a ball of white light. This represents your ascension to your higher power. It also symbolizes the masculine side of your nature — being strong willed, direct, active, assertive, communicative, and competitive. The feminine side is more passive, nurturing, creative, and intuitive. Therefore, you are here on the earth plane to balance yourselves — your masculine side and your feminine side — with gentle strength. Be assertive, yet nurturing. Be strong willed and communicative, yet use your intuition and creativity — all for balance. Of all the twelve paintings, this is the ultimate painting of "divine balance."

As I protect and guard all these paintings, I am especially fond of "The Assumption." For as I guard over Heaven and the other angels, our dear Lady also guards over Heaven. She is the Queen of all that is. Blessed Mother has no power within Herself, meaning that She was a human soul. But Blessed Mother accepted the Holy Call, which I announced to Her through the event of the Annunciation, and She is the Mother of God. She was obedient. She was humble. She was patient. Her heart was filled with unconditional love. Therefore, great honors have been bestowed upon Mary, and She calls Her children to be like Her Son, the Christ, for it is never too late to walk the path of our Lord.

I, Gabriel, send love and great messages, now more than ever, to the earth plane; for I am coming through many visionaries. Angels are manifesting to human beings more than ever before in history, as we reach the close of this age. Know that what I tell you is true, for I am the truth bringer. I send you blessings, love, and regards.

"The Assumption" is painting number ten. This painting's divine energy vibrates with two other paintings in this series. The first is painting number one, "The Annunciation." The number one represents starting over — new beginnings, new foundations. When Mary was assumed into Heaven, She started over and bridged the gap between the physical and the spiritual plane.

The next painting that "The Assumption" aligns with is "The Communion," painting number five. Five plus five equals ten. The Blessed Mother "communed" with the angelic kingdom, with God, the Father, and Her Son, the Christ, when she was assumed into Heaven. Christ also communed with his disciples before the Crucifixion.

The Coronation

Mary's Message

*I, the Blessed Mother of all, am
crowned Queen of Heaven, the angelic
kingdom and the earth. I reign with humility
and gentle grace. I am the Queen of Peace, the
Bright Morning Star. I crown my children with
honor. Receive Christ into your hearts. Accept
this Holy Call. Stand firm in your convictions.
A crown awaits you in Heaven. God's grace be
upon all of His children. He loves you so.*

Description of Painting

Here, Mary is gloriously crowned Queen of Heaven, the angels, and the earth. The crown of twelve stars around her head is ascribed to Mary in the Apocalypse (Book of Revelation).

"The crown is an emblem of victory. Victorious Roman generals returning from war were sometimes presented with a crown or wreath of laurel; winners in contests and races were also crowned with laurel. The crown of gold is worn by kings and queens. We often say, 'You have won the crown of glory. You have overcome sin!'"[11] Stars also represent reunion with our Creator — the highest perfection of glory.

In this painting, the violet-purple light means to heal with gentle love. The pink glow at Mary's heart region shines forth with unconditional love for all Her children. Here, the water at the bottom designates the cosmic flow of change. Change flows through us and raises our soul consciousness to the highest realms of Heaven.

Background
Judith 13:18, 19, 20
Revelation 12:1

"Blessed are You, daughter, by the Most High God, above all the women on earth; and blessed be the Lord God, the Creator of Heaven and earth...Your deed of hope will never be forgotten by those who tell of the might of God. May God make this redound to Your everlasting honor, rewarding You with blessings, because You risked Your life when Your people were being oppressed, and You averted our disaster, walking uprightly before our God." And all the people answered, "Amen! Amen!"

And a great sign appeared in Heaven — a women clothed with the sun, with the moon under Her feet, and on Her head a crown of twelve stars.

Mary's Lesson
The painting, "The Coronation," symbolizes *perseverance*. To persevere means that you must keep on trying. Perseverance demands that you have faith that things will unfold the way they should. Perseverance calls for long-suffering and devotion.

My life on the earth plane was filled with joy and much sorrow, as all of your lives have been. I watched the birth of my newborn Son, Jesus. When they laid Him in my arms, I felt beautiful honor, humility, and love. I watched Him grow. I watched Him blossom, knowing that some day I must release Him — release Him back to His Heavenly Father. But I persevered because I knew there was a calling, and I knew this was a holy blessing and I knew He was our Savior. He was a wonderful man, and He had a wonderful sense of humor. He was gentle and very wise.

I watched Him as He hung on the cross — the darkest hour. I felt every wound and pain, and every cry in agony like a sword piercing my heart. I persevered, knowing that a mother's love knows no bounds; I was called to support and help Him. And so it was.

I ask you all to persevere in life for what is good. Persevere for the truth in your lives. When you read the word of God, know that the path is not easy and the road is not smooth, but God will lift you up lest you dash your foot against a stone. God will lift you up to overcome obstacles in your life. He will make you light of heart.

I encourage you all not to think of suicide. There are many suicides daily. When you destroy your bodies, you dishonor God, for the Lord knows your time of birth, and He knows your time to pass. For everything there is a season and a time for every purpose under Heaven. It is not your right to take your own lives through suicide. You are all here to learn. This earthly plane is your training ground.

I ask you, then, to put on the armor of perseverance. As the good knights of the Middle Ages rode forward in faith and valor, they carried a banner. They rode for Christianity, and in the

Crusades in the 1200s and 1300s, they rode forward in honor and
perseverance for Christianity. I ask all of you — I commend all of
you — to ride forward for the word of God.

Persevere in your beliefs. Persevere for the good. Have patience
to know that all of you were created for a purpose, for a mission.
God knows your mission. If you look within your hearts, through
prayer and meditation, you will find your mission. Every one of
you is special, precious, and loved.

I honor each and every one of you, and I give you a crown, a
crown to wear to know that we all shall be reunited in Heaven,
that each one of you shall receive a crown from God — a crown of
honor — for you are His special children.

When I was crowned Queen of Heaven, of the angelic kingdom,
and of the earth, I remained humble. I have come to you in many
forms, wearing many colors. I have appeared to some of you with
my crown and my scepter; to others, as a humble peasant. All of
these are me, for I am your Queen, I am your Mother. I am the
healing, loving, feminine, divine essence of the world. I am also a
humble one that received a *calling* many centuries ago and agreed
to the calling.

Each of you has a calling. Open your hearts and agree to it and
accept it, for the times now are transitory. Material wealth and success
are fine, but when they override the word of God — when humans
obsess about what they have, who they are, and how they are mea-
suring their value by other peoples' standards — this is not from
God. This is ego. Ego is self-centered. Ego is weak, because ego is
based on the foundation of what others feel, think, and how they
judge a person. Ego also has to do with control. When we place our
lives in God's hands, we let go. Remember, God steers your course if
you let Him. God gives you what you need if you let Him.

I ask each one of you to keep on persevering for what you know is right through the words of the Holy Bible, through what feels right for you in your heart, for what brings you deep joy. The time is coming when your perseverance will be recognized. All of you will stand before the throne of God, with choirs of angels singing, the saints bowing, and the throne illuminated with beautiful light — prismatic light. You will know in your soul that your perseverance has brought you to where you are and where you shall ever remain in our heavenly Kingdom.

Remember the crown — the crown of honor. Forget not to praise your Heavenly Father, for gratitude and thankfulness is very important in prayer time. Thankfulness should be given first. Then, it is good to ask for help, and lastly to listen. Listening is very important, for answers will come to each individual as he or she needs them.

Remember that God works in mysterious ways. His wonders abound. Open your eyes. Open your mind and heart to the wonders of the Lord. I ask all of you to value what is good, to accept what is true, and to turn your back on what is not.

The time is approaching for change, but it is not too late. I extend my hand in gentleness and in hope. Take my hand, for I shall always persevere in your behalf as I did my Son's when I was on the earth plane. I shall ever give you my motherly love, and I ask that you persevere in the name of our Heavenly Father, God the Almighty — whence you have come, my children, and to whom you shall return.

May our Father's blessing fall upon you. May you know peace in your hearts, and may you accept what is good, pure, and holy.

Meditation

We are all heirs to the throne of grace — to God's Kingdom. It was a glorious day when I was crowned "Queen of Heaven." I reign with compassion and grace. A crown awaits you. We are all equal in the eyes of God. We are perfected in His love.

You shall be honored as God's children. My precious ones, I give you your crown. I now place it on your head with reverence. You are special and very important in all that is. Please remember that the Divine awaits you. God knows every deed and thought. By God's grace you deserve the crown and will wear it. Please believe this. If you feel alone and distraught, place the crown on your head. Wear it as our Holy Father wears it, as Christ Jesus wears it, and as I wear it. You are our heirs. Believe — just believe this truth!

Sit quietly and comfortably in a darkened room. Still the mind, and block out any intruding thoughts or sounds. Close your eyes and take a few minutes to deep breathe. My feminine, healing essence is coming to you now. I am handing you your personal crown. This is the crown you will inherit. What does your crown look like? Is it fancy or plain, jeweled or simple? Accept the crown for I am now placing it gently on your head. You are a child of God, a co-creator with God, for God is within you. You shall reign with gentle humility and compassion. You shall honor and show equality to all of humanity and to all kingdoms of the world (mineral, plant, animal). You are now an heir to God's earthly and heavenly Kingdom, as you have always been. How do you feel with your crown well-placed? I love you, as my Son, the Christ, loves you, as your Holy Creator loves you. Please love yourself and be kind to one another.

The Coronation Prayer

Dear Lord God,

We know a crown awaits us in Heaven.

You have promised us salvation, and we believe it!

Blessed are they who have not seen and yet believe.

We know that we need to walk by faith and not by sight.

Let us have greater faith than ever before.

We believe in Your wondrous works, Father.

We believe in our most beautiful, Blessed Virgin Mary,

and we believe in Your Immortal Son, the Christ.

We know You await us in Heaven

and the power of the Trinity is always within us.

Our souls reach up now toward Heaven to receive our crowns.

We will sit immortal and eternally indestructible at the throne of grace.

Praise be to You, Lord.

We thank You for this blessed opportunity to be forever with

You in Your Kingdom.

We believe in all grace that has been given to us

and believe in our salvation.

Thank you, Father, for Your unfailing love and mercy.

Amen.

Archangel Michael on "The Coronation"

I oversee painting number eleven and was assigned to do so because it represents Mary's crowning, Her Coronation into Heaven. I am not only chief of all the archangels, but I am the prince of light in Heaven. Therefore, I came to take Her soul and Her body into Heaven. That is why no remains have been found of our dear, precious Lady. She was raptured and bodily assumed into Heaven. I was there, along with Gabriel, to take Her into my mighty wings and herald Her into the next dimension.

When Mary was crowned Queen of Heaven, which we call the Coronation, Heaven stood still and was reverent. After the great heralding, and joyful singing, there was a great hush as Mary paraded down the middle of the throne room. Her Son Jesus, the Christ, greeted Her, and I was there at Her right arm.

A crown of gold, encrusted with many jewels, was placed on Her head. She bowed and remained quite humble. Mary was chosen for Her humility, Her obedience, and Her acceptance of the Holy Call. She reigns with gentle humility in Heaven, and She loves all Her people.

She appears in "The Coronation" in Her youth, around the age that She bore the Christ. There is an innocence about Her face and humility shows through Her eyes. The pink area at Her heart is aglow for love is pouring from it.

She wears Her golden crown, white dress, and purple robe. The crown represents honor, respect, and eternal divinity. Therefore, I, Michael, the mighty archangel, encourage humanity to step forward and receive their crowns, for a crown awaits each of you in Heaven. This is a painting of hope — to know that all will receive a crown. You shall all rise to the heavenly realms and be in the throne room and then off to your "individual heavens."

The human soul never stops learning and growing; therefore, in Heaven human souls may choose what they want to do. There are many temples of love and learning light, where the energy of the Christ is present. So if you have not learned or been aware of what you needed to do on the earth plane, you can continue to learn in Heaven. There are many, many things to do here. At times you may choose to work with groups of angels to help humanity and to raise the human consciousness of the earth plane. Whatever brings you joy and love will be your unique and particular Heaven.

Know that your life is eternal. Know that you will be with our Lady, along with our gentle Christ, our mighty Creator, the saints and apostles, and all the angels, archangels, and cherubs of Heaven. What a glorious day it will be for us when we receive your soul into Heaven and you enter the throne room to receive your crown.

Forgiveness is the key that opens the door to the throne room in Heaven, along with humility, patience, and gentleness. But dear ones, I, as archangel Michael, want you to know that your sins are forgiven. You do not have to be good to be loved. You do not have to be perfect to be loved. For love judges not. Love is all encompassing. Love forgives. Love sheds any outer skin of intolerance, greed, or cruelty. God is pure white, blinding, unconditional love! Think of that love and put that love into your hearts. For love is the key that opens the door to the throne room. You have been forgiven through what your mighty Savior did for you on the cross. He bore your sins so that you can receive your crown. So I admonish you and again encourage you to have hope in your hearts to know that when you breathe your last breath it is not over, it has only begun.

In this painting our dear, precious, young Mary is looking up. I encourage you all now to look up. Look up and out; see beyond the daily grind. Take time to pray, for prayers are thought forms directed toward your Creator and are very powerful. Know that love *does* heal.

I do not wish to put fear into human hearts, but I want to say that you are approaching a new shift in the physical earth plane. There will be a cataclysm and many weather changes as you have already started to experience. So prayers are very, very healing. There is a "healing energy" throughout the world now, greater than ever before, as we reach the new millennium.

Remember, you are not just human bodies living a *spiritual* life. You are spiritual beings in a human body experiencing a spiritual journey! That is what humanity needs to know. You need to become aware of every thought, of every feeling, of every motivation, of every inclination, and of every intention. You are sparks from God, and God is within you. God is in all creation, even in the air you breathe. Every thought you think procreates with our Creator. So, therefore, the heavenly realms are what you perceive Heaven to be. In my Father's house there are many mansions. What that truly means is there are many, many schools of learning about Christ's teachings, and many, many ways to approach the heavenly realm. In other words, what you think with all the love you have in your heart is what Heaven truly is.

The Book of Revelation describes the throne of God. The throne of God is quite magnificent. God is a source of energy. God is pure unconditional love. God can also manifest in pure blinding light and has done so to human beings on the earth plane before. When souls are heralded into our dimension of Heaven, they meet God face-to-face in the majestic throne room. It is unlike anything any human being has ever seen. It is so high; it is breathtaking. The materials that are used in the throne room are quite glorious — gold, pearl, gemstones, jasper, jade, marble, and many more materials — all unusual, unique, and different. It is not at all austere. It is a room filled with love. It is here that each human soul faces God, falls to his knees in front of the throne, and receives his crown.

Eleven is one of the most powerful numbers; therefore, it vibrates with the painting, "The Coronation." This is a very holy and divine number because it means "as above so below." It represents the heavenly Kingdom coexisting with the earthly kingdom. Mary is crowned Queen of earth, Queen of Heaven, Queen of the angels and the archangels. She rules with gentle dominion. She is the wise and loving Mother of us all.

Eleven is also a perfectly balanced and equal number, with both digits the same; therefore, it represents unity of thought; equality with God; and equality with creation and all that is. It means loving of oneself and knowing of oneself. It is a number of loyalty, and a number of divine intervention and protection.

The Miraculous Medal

Mary's Message

*I, Mary, the
Blessed Mother, appeared
to my daughter, Catherine Labouré
in 1830. She was pure and contrite of heart.
She remained humble throughout her earthly life.
This painting, above all the others, reminds us of
miracles. Miracles happen through earnest and
unshakable faith. Let miracles happen in your life
daily. Do not discount the power of prayer. As
my heart and Christ's bleed for you, we give
you hope. Let miracles fall upon you in
abundance — all who believe. Be healed
in the name of my Son, Jesus Christ.
Blessings on your souls, all who
gaze on these blessed paintings.*

Description of Painting

This portrayal of the Miraculous Medal is the last of the twelve paintings, and represents *miracles*. This portrait of the Madonna is reminiscent of Renaissance portraits. She is set slightly back into space and is seen from a lower point of view so that She appears to look down at the spectator. This gives Mary an aura of impressive elegance.

In Her hand is a golden globe, which means oneness and wholeness with the universal God. It represents unity of all creation, mastery of thought, and it is a power symbol of light, miracles, and new beginnings.

The violet colored vortex above Mary's head signifies a spiritual healing light that permeates the world. The white ball of light at the very top suggests a knowing of blessings to come. The twelve pearls at Her neck mean purity of thought and purpose.

The rose-pink, heart color at the lower right represents Mary's heart pierced with a sword (representing unconditional love); and the circle of color at the left is the heart of Jesus with thorny strokes (meaning wounds shall be healed).

Background

The concept of the Medal of the Immaculate Conception, commonly called the Miraculous Medal, was given to Catherine Labouré in 1830, by an apparition of the Blessed Mother. Catherine, at the time, was a Sister of Charity in Paris, France.

On November 27th, Catherine saw Mary at the altar standing on a globe. In her own words, ". . . A frame formed round the Blessed Virgin, within it was written in gold: *O Mary, conceived without sin, pray for us who have recourse to thee.* Then the voice said 'Have a medal struck after this model. All who wear it will receive great graces'. . ."[12] She continued to describe how the image turned and on the reverse was a large initial "M" surmounted by a bar and cross with the hearts of Jesus and Mary. Jesus' heart was crowned with thorns and Mary's was pierced with a sword. Many miracles have since been obtained by the wearing of the Miraculous Medal.

Mary's Lesson

The twelfth painting, "The Miraculous Medal," symbolizes *miracles*. You are all miracles. You are the creation and thoughts of God. Everything is a miracle: life, nature, the air you breathe. Everything you are is miraculous, for God is a miracle worker and God can create miracles in your life if you let Him.

Open your hearts to our Heavenly Father, for miracles are about to shower upon all of you, changing your lives. A miracle can be small or it can be large, but each individual knows a miracle when he sees one.

Many of you are disabled, physically incapacitated, in pain and suffering. Remember, you shall expect healing miracles and receive them. Expect miracles each day in your life. Look for them; they are all around you.

I appeared to my dear daughter, Catherine, in Paris in 1830 to bring hope to the nations, because humanity always needs signs — physical, tangible evidence — that God exists and that miracles abound. In war torn times especially, you need to know and believe in miracles.

Catherine accepted the call to move my wishes forward. In a vision, I showed her my essence and showed her how the Miraculous Medal should look. I told Catherine, "My dear daughter, the ones who wear it shall receive blessings from

Heaven." Many blessings *were* bestowed upon mankind, and still are today.

Whether you are Catholic or not, I encourage you to carry a Miraculous Medal, or to wear one. There is power behind this medal. In the twelve paintings, there are scriptural titles, and there are events from the Bible, but "The Miraculous Medal" stands alone. I chose it to be the twelfth painting because it represents all the good that there is in the form of miraculous love — miraculous caring for each of you.

Pray for miracles, and pray also to do the Lord's will; not your own self-centered will, but to do the will of your Father in Heaven. "Not my will but Thine be done" should be prayed daily. Ask our Lord to show you what His will is for your life.

Love produces miracles. Faith and hope produce miracles, as does the word of God — the truth. Reading the Bible will instill within your heart a foundation — a foundation of love and God's word that will produce miracles.

I have appeared in many ways, to many people. I am especially well pleased with the Miraculous Medal, the words inscribed on it and the meaning behind it.

My heart was many times symbolically pierced with a sword, through what I endured and, of course, through what my Son endured. He was able to rise above; He overcame death for eternal life. I overcame death as I was assumed into Heaven. So shall all of you overcome death. Life is a miracle, but death is also a miracle; because death transports us from a physical realm to a heavenly realm, where we will live eternally blessed in God's grace.

Remember, there are infinite miracles awaiting you. Open your eyes to see miracles daily. Saint Catherine, or Catherine Labouré, was called on a mission. I chose her because she remained humble throughout her lifetime as I remained humble, and she persevered as I persevered with our Lord.

I am asking all of you to find your true mission. You were all sent here on a mission. You all have a calling. That is a miracle in itself. You are all seeds, planted to extend your roots — your tender roots — one to another; to reach out and to give light to humanity. Remember, he that hides his light under a bushel becomes darkened inside. Therefore, find your talents and ask God to show them to you if you do not know them already. Use them wisely for the glory of God.

Use your gifts, my children, wisely — for the glory of God. Whatever gifts they may be — healing, prophecy, discernment — use them wisely for humanity. We all have gifts and talents. We need to ask God to show us where we belong and what we need to be doing.

This twelfth painting also represents completion. Upon your passing to the heavenly realm, remember that your birth was a miracle, but also your passing is a miracle. To overcome the shadow of death, and to live eternally forgiven — in a state of love, laughter, joy, peace — this is truly a miracle!

Think about miracles. Take a blank sheet of paper and write down five miracles that you would like in your life. Ask God in His divine wisdom to help you discern what miracles you truly want, and to show you what miracles are for your highest good. Whatever brings you peace, whatever uplifts you and ennobles you, is a miracle from God.

We all need healing. Remember to touch and love your inner child. Remember to share what is good, one to another; be in communion with each other.

The Lord of Lights, our Heavenly Father, sends you all blessings — sends you all good things. Work for Him the short days of your lives. Work for His glory, His honor, and His majesty. He shall not forget you at the end time. Be good soldiers moving forward with the truth. Ask for miracles, but also give miracles to other people: give your time, your energy, and your talents, for there is not a human being that does not need an encouraging word or help in some form.

I have given many signs throughout these centuries. These paintings are one of the signs, for I know that humanity needs tangible signs to look at and to evaluate. As the Miraculous Medal was a tangible, enduring, and everlasting sign, so are these paintings. I want you to accept them with an open mind. I, the Blessed Mother, have ordained these paintings, and I tell you that miracles will occur when people view them.

Miracles come in many forms. They can be accepted as healing miracles, emotional miracles, spiritual miracles; but people will know in their hearts when a miracle occurs for them.

So I am asking you — my children, my people — to remain open to these works for these are a sign from me that there is hope and that there will be many miracles bestowed upon the masses, for I am not just for one individual or one group. I, the Blessed Mother, am Mother of all — in all religions, in all towns and cities of the world, in any place where you are, and in any condition that you are in.

I am your Mother, your Heavenly Mother. I love you as my own, and I bring you into my heart to remain there always. I reach out my hand. Please, take it. Pray. I will intercede for you. Do what is good. Say the rosary. Carry or wear the Miraculous Medal. Pray; meditate; love one another; love yourselves; love God and creation; be gentle one to another, rebuking not; be patient; be humble.

Glory awaits you, my children. I am well pleased with those who have lifted their cross and carried it, looking to the mark which is my Son, the Christ — looking ahead. It is fine to look back over your life and reflect, but remember to keep looking ahead; my Son, the Shepherd, will mark your path. He will guide you, direct you. He will take you into our Father's Kingdom.

There will also be other signs for humanity. Be open to what is good, pure, true, and holy. I love you, my precious children. God loves you. My Son, the Christ, loves you. Blessings and miracles be upon you daily, now and forever more.

Meditation

There will be many more visions, apparitions, and signs of my presence in days to come. My essence will be portrayed in many forms. As the Miraculous Medal was struck and proved to be a permanent sign for miracles, so shall other signs occur and be permanent.

This painting is the last of the twelve. It represents perfect alignment for us. My heart and the heart of Jesus are in balance with the beating hearts of the world. I hold the golden globe for containment of the highest thoughts and ideals of the Creator. I wear my pearls of purity for you, so you shall know that all your tears have turned to pearls. I gave myself unconditionally to the request of my Higher Power — the godhead. We simply ask humanity for reverence, respect, love, compassion, and honor. Honor your Creator, yourselves, and others. Think about living a Christ-like life. Think of my mothering, nurturing gentleness.

Relax your mind and body. Sit comfortably straight and uncross your legs. Sit with your hands on your lap, palms up. Take five or six deep breaths and when you are done, close your eyes. See a room in your mind. You are standing in a very special room. Look at your room in detail. What does your room look like? Is it large or small? What shape is it? This is the inner sanctum or the chamber of your heart. This is where miracles start, through love and faith. Now visualize a medal somewhere in your room. Where is it located? What shape is it? What material is it made of? Gaze upon your medal. This is your Miraculous Medal. This is a holy and powerful medal for it vibrates with the beautiful energy of God. Be enveloped with your own Miraculous Medal. Through the power of God's anointing, you release anything that is unlike God. The medal is your point of contact for release.

Now, think of a miracle that you would like to have manifested in your life today. Say to yourself, "This day I will experience a miracle regarding _____." (Fill in the blank.) When you are in need of a miracle, pray to your Heavenly Creator, in the name of my Son, the Christ, and visualize your Miraculous Medal. This is a divine, personal symbol from God to you.

May God's greatest peace and grace be upon all of you.

The Miraculous Medal Prayer

Dear Lord, we believe in miracles!

By Your divine grace and love we receive them.

Let there be miracles today in our lives.

We now expect miracles in all the areas that we need them.

Send Your angels of healing and hope into our lives today.

Let miracles fall upon us as the gentle rains from Heaven.

Let us remember to revere all life — for it is a miracle.

Let us be aware and see good in everything and everyone.

Though our hearts, at times, might be pierced with emotional wounds,

and our bodies and minds with physical pain,

we believe in Your goodness and mercy.

We receive openly all that is good, pure, and holy.

Hold us in the palm of Your hand, Dear Father.

Let blessings fall upon us and shower us with all good things.

Let us not forget to share Your divine gifts

and our personal gifts and talents with others.

Keep us close to Your bosom, in prayer time and protection.

Praise be to God, our Creator!

The Creator of infinite miracles, be with us, in us, and for us,

now and forever.

Amen.

Archangel Gabriel on "The Miraculous Medal"

I, Gabriel, am the angel of revelation. I deliver and interpret visions. This painting is a symbol of divine visions. The Miraculous Medal, worn by those who cherish our Blessed Mother, came from a vision.

There was a beautiful lady in Paris, France named Catherine Labouré. Like Mary, she also was gentle, humble of heart and obedient. She loved the Christ dearly, and wanted to become the bride of Christ. She joined the Sisters of Charity in Paris. Her father grew angry when she did not marry into a wealthy family. She was devout her entire life, and had many visions and apparitions of our Lady, angels, and the Christ. Before each apparition or vision, I would appear. For as I said, I deliver and interpret visions — I am the angel of revelations.

Blessed Mother appeared to Catherine many times during her life. One time, in 1830, She requested Catherine do something for Her and humanity. Catherine entered the chapel and heard a swish of silk, which represented our Lady's presence. When she turned, she saw our Lady standing beside the altar. Each finger emanated a different ray of color — for our Lady was wearing a different gemstone on each finger. This represented balance for the world: that all nations, peoples, communities, neighborhoods, and races would live in harmony and peace — one to the other. As Catherine looked in awe she saw an oval forming around the Blessed Mother, with words written on the outside edge. They said, "O Mary, conceived without sin, pray for us who have recourse to Thee." Mary was standing on a golden globe which represented the unification of the world. As Mary slowly turned around, the oval moved with Her, and Mary proceeded to show Catherine how the back of the medal should look. There was a cross on the back. Beneath the cross was an "M" for Mary, with a horizontal bar along the "M". Beneath the "M" initial were the sacred hearts of Mary and Jesus. These symbols were surrounded by twelve stars.

The Blessed Mother has appeared with a crown of twelve stars in some other apparitions. In the Book of Revelation, there is a passage which states, "She is clothed with the sun, standing on the moon and has a crown of twelve stars." This truly represents our Lady, the Blessed Mother, Mary.

Catherine went and told the Bishop that Mary wanted a medal created for humanity. Later, he also had an apparition, which convinced him to have the medal struck in 1832. Catherine carried the secret with her until a few months before she passed away. After being encouraged by the bishop to tell humanity who indeed saw the original apparition, Catherine disclosed how she communicated with Blessed Mother, what she saw, and then breathed her last breath.

The medal was first called the Medal of the Immaculate Conception. Today, it is called the Miraculous Medal. Believe me my children, it is not just for Catholics! It is a very powerful medal, because contained within it are the graces of our Lady — the powerful cross of the Christ, the hearts of unconditional love, and the stars.

This twelfth painting shows the essence of Mary, with the superimposed facial features of Catherine, Her dearly beloved daughter who is now with Mary in Heaven. In this beautiful paint-ing, Mary holds the golden globe which represents unity and one-ness for your world and humanity. There is a vortex of purple light that rises above the golden globe. This symbolizes your higher soul-conscious mind. Remember, purple vibrates with the seat of intuition — our godhead connection. The heart on the right, (as the viewer sees it), is the heart of our Blessed Mother — pierced with a sword; for Her heart cries and is wounded for those who have not believed. The heart on your left is the sacred heart of Jesus — surrounded by thorny strokes. The cross prevails over this heart. The cross at our Lady's throat represents the truth — to speak what is for your highest good. The twelve pearls around Her neck symbolize purity of purpose and tears that have been shed. The tears have turned into a thing of beauty, for all tears in Heaven will be cleansed and become as pearls.

This is a self-empowering painting. It is a painting of true balance, and it denotes the completion of a spiritual journey. For at the end of each journey, one of the greatest of miracles is performed — that of eternal life! You will go from the dense material and physical world and transcend into a world of light, color, love, and beauty. Be reassured of all of this as you look at these gentle blue eyes, (remember St. Catherine Labouré's eyes are superimposed over Mary's.)

This is a project of heart love, light, and God's divine ordination. So, I, Gabriel — as the angel of the Annunciation, the Resurrection, revelation, and visions — encourage you to look at the painting of "The Miraculous Medal" and to buy a medal and carry it with you. I admonish you to stay in your prayer time, to be gentle with yourselves, to walk and speak your own truth, to find your true mission, to balance all areas of your life, to believe in miracles and in love, to release your inner child in joy and light. Remember, miracles start within the heart through faith and love.

Many will receive miracles from the viewing of these paintings. Crutches will fall to the ground. Spirits will soar. Believe, children, *just believe*. The archangels and the angels of Heaven send you what you need. The Christ and our Lady send you divine love, and our Heavenly Father guards and protects your souls now and always.

─────────

Painting number twelve, "The Miraculous Medal," represents miracles. This is a summation of all the paintings. Miracles will fall upon human beings from the heavenly realms to the earthly plane. There will be miracles in the minds, bodies, and hearts of the people that imbibe the paintings and read the lessons, messages, and prayers.

Twelve is a number of completion, and it represents completing a task, a project, or a journey. As you know there are twelve numbers on the face of a clock. When the clock chimes from midnight to one o'clock in the morning, it is a new day. There are twelve months of the year. When December ends, it is a new year as we start into January.

Our Lady requested that the "Miraculous Medal" be in the twelfth position, for it is the completion painting of this divine project, and the new beginning of great miracles for humanity.

Epilogue

On June 30, 1997, I had a vision before I awakened. In it I heard a knock on the door. It was a very loud knock, which startled me, and I began to awaken (in my vision). I was in the home I grew up in — the one my father built. I was at the top of the staircase. At the bottom of the stairs was the Blessed Mother, all in white. She looked up at me, and in Her left hand She had a white dove whose wings were fluttering. With Her right hand She beckoned me to come down the steps. I gasped when I saw Her — for it was so real. From behind her stepped my earthly mother, Dorothy. She also put out her right hand and beckoned me to come down the stairs.

I slept on, and promptly at 9:00 A.M., I heard a clicking sound! I thought my husband had set the alarm, but it wasn't the alarm. The ceiling fan overhead was changing direction! Then the light came on very brightly, followed by the light on my headboard!

It was the last day of June, symbolic of a time of completion. Every date has been significant during this project. There are no coincidences. I am always aware of promptings from spirit. This meant this was the day that the conclusions would be given for *Visions from Mary*.

I went to my office and proceeded to dictate (from the Blessed Mother) the following into my tape recorder:

The conclusion for painting number 1, "The Annunciation," is this: Remember our Creator loves you, our Creator created you, you need to give praise and glory to our Creator. You need to announce your truth to yourselves, to others and to the Creator. You need to have discernment in your lives. You need to be honest with yourselves before you can be honest with others. This is a time of great awakening. Many new things will be announced to humanity through my presence and through the presence of the Holy Spirit — through signs, through wonders. Prepare yourselves now in reverence and humility. Remember that you were created to be divine beings. Honor yourselves, honor others, and honor your Creator.

The conclusion for the rest of the paintings is that these are paintings of love, healing, and empowerment. Miracles will occur through the viewing of the paintings, and through the prayers that will be said while viewing each painting. Use daily, the meditations I have given you for each painting. These are tools for balance, alignment, emotional and physical healing, and spiritual development.

I have sent these paintings — all twelve — through my daughter, Michele. Again, she was chosen for her childlike spirit. Unless we become as children, we cannot enter the Kingdom of Heaven. A child sees through the eyes of wonder, acceptance, and unconditional love. I call you to become as children in your hearts. Love one another, and accept one another. These are paintings of preparation. You are now to prepare yourselves for the return of my Son, the Christ; prepare yourselves for your rapture. The Creator wishes abundance for all of your lives. As the new millennium approaches, many miracles will occur. These are sent from our Divine Creator, our God. Accept the miracles daily that come your way. Look for them, feel that you deserve them, and give thanks for them.

The year 2000 will be very pivotal for humanity. For many, many thousands will come to the light. They will come to the belief in knowing that there is the heavenly beyond. The reign of darkness will end. There is new hope for all. Remember, *to forgive* is one of the most healing elements in the universe. Remember *to love*. Remember *to pray*. Remember *to be joyful* and *to be thankful*. Be happy as little children — one to another, respecting one another, giving and sharing with one another. The path will never be easy on the earthly plane, but know that your earthly life is just a transition, that your soul is eternal, that it is indestructible, that we shall all be reunited in that heavenly dimension of lights!

Read the words I have given you. Reflect upon their meaning, for the divine, healing energy of the Mother love comes through the paintings. Remember, they are not of my physical appearance as I appeared before. They are symbolic, and they are the essence of the mother love — of the divine, nurturing, healing spirit that permeates through and in all of you. So I beckon you to have a healing wherever you need a healing in your life.

Pray for your lives to be in balance on all planes of existence. Pray for your fellow man, for the world, and for all souls to be saved. Pray for those that have passed on. They also need prayers. Pray for the lost, the disillusioned, and the desolate. I beseech you to open up your hearts and let the love and the light of my Son, the Christ, pour in. Let your lives be changed. Again, read these words that I have given you. Pray the prayers, the meditations. *Listen*, and read my messages. Accept these as a sign of unification and healing for humanity. For as surely as there have been miracles, there shall be many, many more healings from the viewing of these paintings, from the reading of my words, and from the honoring of our Creator, and my Son, the Christ, who died for you. I send blessings into each and every life. I pray for beautiful petals of roses to fall upon you in miraculous ways, in ways of great healings.

The time has come *now* to take a stand for the truth. There is truth in each and every painting that was created from my essence through my daughter, Michele. This shall be found to be true. Accept these works that I have given you with open hearts, with open minds. I love you, my dear children. May the grace of God be upon you. May the love of His heavenly Kingdom be ahead of you. May His unconditional love of all creation be in your heart. May you find inner peace. Know that there is hope. The new millennium houses the age of hope. You are coming now to a close of a thousand years. The time is at hand now to prepare for the upcoming millennium. God's blessings be upon you.

Mary, the Blessed Mother

Archangels Epilogue

As my communication with the archangels concluded, on July 14, 1998, I realized what an overwhelming amount of information had been conveyed. It was done so with love and dedication for God, the Christ, and the Blessed Mother. The archangels took their jobs very seriously, and I ultimately could feel their love and concern for all of God's children.

Daniel, my project angel of inspiration and creative writing, once again appeared before the archangels entered the room on the final morning of our communication. He said,

> *You are loved. May peace be among you and remain in your heart. Now, I will step aside and let archangel Michael come through.*
>
> *Hark, my beloved child Michele, my namesake. This is archangel Michael. I am here today to talk about the paintings. Do not lose hope. The twelve paintings are divinely ordained and blessed. Remember, there were also twelve tribes of Israel and twelve disciples. Our Lady Mary sends love and regards.*

With that, archangel Michael stepped aside and the Blessed Mother appeared.

As I saw Mary that day, She looked very young, about the age of sixteen. She had a very, very clear complexion, slightly rosy cheeks, and beautiful light-colored eyes. Her chestnut brown hair was parted in the middle and fell behind Her shoulders. She wore her white tunic, the blue mantle, and sandals. Then she spoke:

> *Hello, my child. I am very pleased with this project. I did not want to overwhelm you in the beginning; therefore, I chose to let the archangels come through at the very end.*

There is much information that has been given. All of it is true. There is one holy God, and there are many messengers; I am a messenger; my Son, the Christ, is a messenger; and the angels and archangels are messengers. You, too, daughter, are a messenger for the divine Holy Spirit.

Paintings one through twelve are meant to evoke different emotional responses. Each person who views these paintings will receive divine anointing. The love of God will come through the paintings. My healing essence, care, and concern for humanity will emanate through the paintings.

I come to you as a young girl, because this is how I appeared to Gabriel as he conversed with me for the first couple of years before I conceived the Christ. Archangel Michael is my right arm; and yes, he does herald me into the third dimension, which is the earth plane. He is a mighty warrior, and he is the prince of light and peace in Heaven. Archangel Gabriel is the ultimate messenger. He (or she), I send forth at times to deliver good news to the world. And, of course, we must not forget archangel Raphael, the divine archangel of healing. These archangels were hand chosen and selected to guard, oversee, protect, and vibrate with the four paintings that each of them have described. This was designated many centuries ago.

Today, I bring you blessings, miracles, love, and good tidings. Know that a crown awaits you in Heaven through perseverance, and that miracles fall upon those obedient unto the call.

When She finished speaking, Mary faded into a ball of pure white light and disappeared. Archangel Michael then appeared and spoke to me:

When individuals view these paintings, they will receive the virtue of each painting and take it into their hearts. All twelve contain what humanity needs now, by the virtues emanating from each painting. Everyone needs to:

Remain humble *in heart*

Show the world unconditional love

Regard each other with respect *and* esteem

Cleanse *what is no longer for your highest good*

Unite *in unity, one to the other with sharing and caring*

Forgive *others and also to* forgive *yourselves*

Renew faith *and* hope *on your daily walk*

Know *that you are* redeemed *each day*

Reflect upon the gifts of the spirit, *and pray that they descend upon you so that you can be more God-like*

Love *Mary, our Holy Mother, remembering Her mission and Her Call, and revere Her accepting that call*

Persevere *along a spiritual path*

Expect *miracles in your lives*

Revere *the earth and all that is upon it*

A single painting may not heal you, but together the twelve will bring goodness to all. Many blessings will be bestowed upon the individual who reads the lessons and views the paintings with an open mind and an open heart.

Appendix A

The Rosary

Mary frequently mentions the rosary throughout this book. The rosary is not just for Catholics. Mary urges everyone, no matter what their faith, to pray the rosary. Saying the rosary brings us closer in meditation to Mary and Her Son, Jesus. This spiritual practice inspires faith, hope, and confidence.

According to the booklet, *The Rosary Crusade*, by the Dominican Fathers, "Rosary is derived from the Latin word 'rosarium,' meaning a garden of roses, and was used as far back as the thirteenth century. Mary's favorite flower is the rose, so what a befitting name. The rosary, containing one hundred and fifty Hail Mary's, or Angelic salutations, is sometimes called the Psalter of Mary, in imitation of the one hundred and fifty Psalms of David contained in the Bible."[13]

The total rosary involves reciting a series of introductory prayers; reciting fifteen decades of Hail Mary along with accompanying prayers; and, contemplating each of the fifteen mysteries. One completes three trips around the circular array of beads. Most people, though, recite five decades in one sitting, making one complete circuit around the beads.[14]

The first five Mysteries are called the Joyful Mysteries and pertain to five events that occurred before Christ's crucifixion. The Sorrowful Mysteries are meditations surrounding the Crucifixion. The Glorious Mysteries are based on experiences which occurred after the Crucifixion. (See the rosary diagram and prayers of the rosary listed in appendix B.)

Even though I personally say the rosary, I did not think to include them in any detail in this book, until I began receiving signs about its importance. For about two weeks prior to Christmas 1998, I received many gifts pertaining to the rosary. One was a beautiful porcelain locket of the Nativity with the Hail Mary inscribed on the back. Then, on Christmas Eve, Mary visited me in a vision. She looked resplendent and was wearing a gold crown. Mary indeed appeared as the Queen of Peace. Surrounding Her was brilliant blue light tinged with rose pink. Around Her neck was a large gold crucifix and rosary beads of large pearls. Mary said, "Daughter, I want you to adapt the concept of the rosary to use with my paintings. The first five decades correlate with the first five paintings. As you are saying the ten Hail Mary's for each painting, think of the painting's virtue. The first five recitations are to be called the *Primary Meditations*."

She explained that these correspond with the first five paintings, four of which refer to biblical events, and the fifth, (painting number two), which refers to a title bestowed upon Mary.

1. "The Annunciation" — Humility
2. "The Mystical Rose" — Unconditional Love
3. "The Nativity" — Esteem of Spiritual Values
4. "The Baptism" — Purification and Renewal
5. "The Communion" — Unity and Oneness

The *Secondary Meditations* coincide with paintings six through ten. Again, as you are saying the Hail Mary's, think of the virtue of that painting and imbibe it:

6. "The Crucifixion" — Forgiveness
7. "The Resurrection" — Faith and Hope
8. "Lamb of God" — Redemption
9. "The Descent of the Holy Spirit"
   — The Nine Gifts of the Spirit
10. "The Assumption" — Devotion to Mary

Mary instructed me to call the last set of five the *Triune Mediations*. In addition to the final two paintings, She tells us to concentrate on the Trinity — Father, Son, and Holy Spirit.

The first ten Hail Mary's are said while viewing painting number eleven, "The Coronation." Here, we are to ponder upon perseverance. During the next decade, view painting number twelve, "The Miraculous Medal," while meditating on miracles. For the remaining decades, the Blessed Mother asks us to focus first upon our loving God — the Creator; next upon Christ, our Savior, who died for us; and, finally upon the infinite power of the Holy Spirit. By doing so we will more fully embrace "one in all" and the power and love of the Holy Trinity.

Appendix B
The Fifteen Mysteries of the Rosary

The Five Joyful Mysteries

1. The Annunciation — The Angel Gabriel announces to the Virgin Mary that God wishes her to become the Mother of His Son. Mary obeys with humility.
2. The Visitation — Mary visits St. Elizabeth, who is to be mother of St. John the Baptist. She assists Elizabeth for three months.
3. The Birth of Christ — Jesus Christ, the Son of God, is born in a stable. His Mother places Him in a manger. Shepherds and wise men visit Him.
4. The Presentation — Mary and Joseph take the Child Jesus to the Temple at Jerusalem to present Him to His Heavenly Father.
5. The Finding of the Child Jesus in the Temple — Having lost Jesus, Mary, and Joseph seek Him. After three days they find Him in the Temple.

The Five Sorrowful Mysteries

1. The Agony in the Garden — Jesus prays in the Garden of Olives. The thought of His coming sufferings and of our sins causes him to sweat blood.
2. The Scourging at the Pillar — Jesus is stripped, bound to a pillar, and scourged until His body is covered with wounds and blood.
3. The Crowning with Thorns — A crown of thorns is pressed into the head of Jesus. His eyes fill with tears and blood. He is mocked and spat upon.
4. The Carrying of the Cross — Jesus carries His heavy cross to Calvary. Mary makes the stations of the cross with Her suffering Son.

5. The Crucifixion — Nailed to the cross, Jesus, after three hours of agony, dies in the presence of His Mother.

The Five Glorious Mysteries

1. The Resurrection — Victorious over death, Jesus rises from the grave, glorious and immortal, on Easter Sunday. He reopens the gates of Heaven.
2. The Ascension — Forty days after His Resurrection, Jesus ascends, in the presence of His Mother and His disciples, into Heaven.
3. The Descent of the Holy Spirit — Ten days after the Ascension, the Holy Spirit descends in tongues of fire upon Mary and the disciples.
4. The Assumption of Mary into Heaven — Mary, Mother of God, was taken body and soul into heavenly glory after the course of Her earthly life.
5. The Crowning of Mary as Queen of Heaven — The Mother of God, to the joy of all the angels and saints, is crowned Queen of Heaven by Her Son.

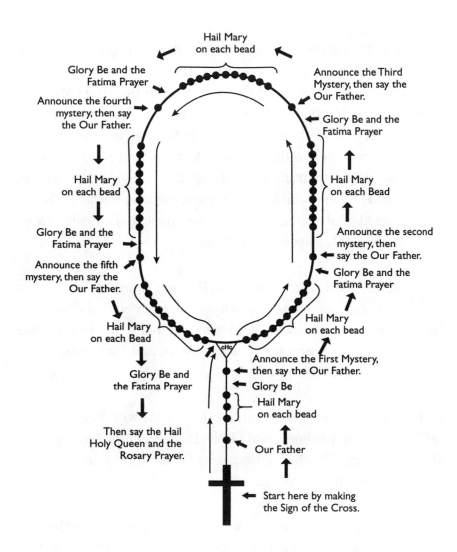

Hail Mary
on each bead

Glory Be and the
Fatima Prayer

Announce the fourth
mystery, then say
the Our Father.

Hail Mary
on each bead

Glory Be and the
Fatima Prayer

Announce the fifth
mystery, then say the
Our Father.

Hail Mary
on each Bead

Glory Be and
the Fatima Prayer

Then say the Hail
Holy Queen and the
Rosary Prayer.

Announce the Third
Mystery, then say the
Our Father.

Glory Be and the
Fatima Prayer

Hail Mary
on each Bead

Announce the second
mystery, then
say the Our Father.

Glory Be and the
Fatima Prayer

Hail Mary
on each bead

Announce the First Mystery,
then say the Our Father.

Glory Be

Hail Mary
on each bead

Our Father

Start here by making
the Sign of the Cross.

Appendix C
The Prayers of the Rosary

Apostles' Creed I believe in God, the Father Almighty, Creator of Heaven and earth; and in Jesus Christ, His only Son, our Lord; Who was conceived by the Holy Spirit, born of the Virgin Mary, suffered under Pontius Pilate, was crucified, died, and was buried. He descended into hell; the third day He arose again from the dead; He ascended into Heaven, sitteth at the right hand of God, the Father Almighty; from thence He shall come to judge the living and the dead. I believe in the Holy Spirit, the holy Catholic Church, the communion of saints, the forgiveness of sins, the resurrection of the body, and life everlasting. Amen.

Our Father. Our Father, Who art in Heaven, hallowed be Thy name; Thy Kingdom come; Thy will be done, on earth as it is in Heaven. Give us this day our daily bread; and forgive us our trespasses as we forgive those who trespass against us; and lead us not into temptation; but deliver us from evil. Amen.

Hail Mary. Hail Mary, full of grace, the Lord is with Thee. Blessed art Thou amongst women, and blessed is the fruit of Thy womb, Jesus. Holy Mary, Mother of God, pray for us sinners now and at the hour of our death. Amen.

Gloria. Glory be to the Father, and to the Son, and to the Holy Spirit as it was in the beginning, is now, and ever shall be, world without end. Amen.

Fatima Prayer. After each decade or mystery of the rosary say the following prayer requested by the Blessed Virgin at Fatima: "O my Jesus, forgive us our sins, save us from the fires of hell, lead all souls to Heaven, especially those most in need of your mercy."

Hail Holy Queen. Hail Holy Queen, Mother of Mercy, our life, our sweetness and our hope! To Thee do we cry, poor banished children of Eve; to Thee do we send up our sighs, mourning and weeping in this valley of tears! Turn then, most gracious Advocate, Thine eyes of mercy towards us, and after this, our exile, show unto us the blessed fruit of Thy womb, Jesus. O clement, O loving, O sweet Virgin Mary! Pray for us, O Holy Mother of God, that we may be made worthy of the promises of Christ.

Rosary Prayer. O God, Whose only begotten Son, by His life, death and resurrection, has purchased for us the rewards of eternal life, grant we beseech Thee, that meditating upon these mysteries in the most holy rosary of the Blessed Virgin Mary, we may imitate what they contain, and obtain what they promise, through the same Christ, our Lord. Amen.

Bibliography

Introduction by G. Scott Sparrow

1. E. Shillebeeckx and C. Halkes, Mary: Yesterday, Today, Tomorrow (New York: Crossroads, 1993), p. 51.

2. J. Ashton. *Mother of All Nations* (New York: Harper and Row, 1989) p. 188.

3. J. M. Haffert. *The Meaning of Akita* (Asbury, New Jersey: 101 Foundation, 1989), p. 23.

4. See R. Faricy, Foreword in J.T. Connell, *Meetings with Mary: Visions of the Blessed Mother* (New York: Ballantine, 1995).

5. See A. Kirkwood, *Mary's Messages to the World* (New York: Putnam, 1995).

6. John 2:3-5.

7. Sparrow, G.S. *I Am With You Always: True Stories of Encounters with Jesus* (New York: Bantam, 1995), p. 202.

Visions from Mary

1. Semmler, Nerius, Rev. *Emblems of Excellence.* New York: The Catholic Information Society, 1944. p. 10.

2. Ibid p. 4.

3. The Mystical Rose Home Page. This website provides an interesting, in-depth study of the origin and history of the Mystical Rose or Rosa Mystica title for the Blessed Mother. (The best way to find this website is to input "Mystical Rose" in the search engine. This should provide Mystical Rose or the Mystical Rose Home Page as one of the results.)

4. *Emblems of Excellence.* p. 8.

5. Ibid p. 8.

6. Ibid p. 5-6.

7. Ibid p. 7-8.

8. Ibid p. 7.

9. Ibid p. 5.

10. The Reverand Oblate Fathers. *The Shrine Prayer Book.* Belleville, Illinois: Shrine of Our Lady of the Snows, 1980. p. 133-136.

11. *Emblems of Excellence.* p. 10.

12. Perpetual Novena. *Our Lady of the Miraculous Medal,* Philadelphia, PA: The Central Association of the Miraculous Medal, 1994. p. 11-12.

13. See The Dominican Fathers. *The Rosary Crusade.* New York: National Head Quarters Holy Name Society, 1943.

14. Sparrow, G. Scott, Ed.D. *Blessed Among Women.* New York: Harmony Books, 1998. p. 262-263.

Michele Livingston

Michele Livingston is an internationally known artist, counselor, and healer. Her artwork is represented in private and corporate collections throughout the United States, Europe, and Asia. Michele has a master's degree in Art Education and has taught art in the public schools and private instruction. For six years, she owned her own art gallery, "Divine Inspirations."

Today, she is an ordained minister who uses her "visionary" capacities to help humanity. While counseling clients, Michele uses the gifts of *prophecy* and *anointing of healing*, two of the nine biblical "gifts of the Holy Spirit." She lives in Camp Hill, Pennsylvania, with her husband Jon Robert Stroh.

The Paintings from *Visions from Mary*

The most remarkable features of the book, *Visions from Mary*, are the twelve paintings created through Michele Livingston by the Blessed Mother. These paintings are of Mother Mary's divine, healing essence, rather than Her actual physical appearance.

Each of the paintings represents a particular healing virtue, and each of you will be drawn to one or more of the paintings — based on the healing required in your life at the time.

All are available as 8" x 10" prints (along with their prayers) ready for framing.

Prices are $9.95 each, or you may buy any three prints for $25.00 plus shipping and handling.

All twelve are available for only $79.95 plus shipping and handling

Larger sizes will be available. E-mail us at: michele@maryvisions.com for further details, or write to us at:

Divine Inspirations
8 Accent Circle
Camp Hill, Pa 17011-1021

A course derived from this book is being formulated as we go to press. If you have interest in attending the course or wish to sponsor the course in your area, please contact us.

About Blue Mantle

We at Blue Mantle Publishing believe that there is a need for something in between self-publishing and advance-paying publishers. We call it "bridge" publishing.

It works like this: If an author believes in his work, but cannot get a royalty-paying publisher to buy it, he can approach Blue Mantle through his agent, or directly. At that point, we review the manuscript to be sure it exhibits high quality and conforms with our publishing ideals.

Then, once we accept the project, we endeavor to work with the author on making any revisions that might be necessary. Then we edit it, lay it out, commission artwork, have it printed, and conduct a lean and mean publicity campaign. We pursue distribution for the work, sell it over the Internet, write press releases, and coach the author on exploiting local media and booksellers. In exchange for this package of services, the author pays for some of our up-front costs, and then Blue Mantle thereafter owns a percentage of the book's gross sales. These figures are negotiated, and entered into a contract between the author and Blue Mantle. Then, upon the "platform" of greater visibility and credibility created by this approach, we will actively assist the author in presenting the book to one of the major publishers through a New York agency or through our own contacts in the publishing field. It the manuscript sells, with or without our assistance, then Blue Mantle — as a co-owner — shares in the sale of the book at a contracted percentage of advance and royalties.

The twelve color prints in the back of this book are perforated so that they can be easily removed. This will enable the reader to view them as they study the chapters.

The Annunciation

The Mystical Rose

The Nativity

The Baptism

The Communion

The Crucifixion

The Resurrection

The Lamb of God

The Descent of the Holy Spirit

The Assumption

The Coronation

The Miraculous Medal